Happy Hanukkah Love Mom — wishing
you a year of laughter, starting
tonight.

Love,
Me

the five jerks
you meet on earth

the five jerks
you meet on earth

RAY ZARDETTO

**Andrews McMeel
Publishing, LLC**
Kansas City

06 07 08 09 10 RR2 10 9 8 7 6 5 4 3 2 1

ISBN-13: 978-0-7407-6082-2
ISBN-10: 0-7407-6082-3

Library of Congress Control Number: 2006923260

www.andrewsmcmeel.com

ATTENTION: SCHOOLS AND BUSINESSES

Andrews McMeel books are available at quantity discounts with bulk purchase for educational, business, or sales promotional use. For information, please write to: Special Sales Department, Andrews McMeel Publishing, LLC, 4520 Main Street, Kansas City, Missouri 64111.

To my family, Rita, Gina,
Joey, and Montana;
may you enjoy
your rights and privileges.

contents

the five jerks
you meet on earth

al mitchell

AL MITCHELL WAS a quality guy without a quality life.

He played by the rules: good grades in school, worked hard, honored his father and his mother. He was honest—well, with the exception of those few liberties he took on his taxes and the exaggerations on his résumé—but who didn't do that? Anyone would tell you Al was steadfast, loyal, and imaginative. So how could it be that Al stood on the brink of middle age with a life as empty as a theater hosting a Paris Hilton film festival?

Perhaps it was his sense of priorities. They were always a little off. When he was ten, Al obsessed on the earliest generation of video games while the rest of his friends joined Little League.

When the baseball bug finally bit hard in his teenage years, Al found that his friends were turning their attention to girls, cars, and the Jersey Shore, leaving Al alone to bat his balls.

Not that this bothered Al very much. Being alone was easy and stress-free. Besides, he never did make friends easily or suffer foolish company gladly.

As they grew older, Al's friends filled their weekends at the Jersey Shore—the Seafarer Beach and Boardwalk, to be specific. Because Al worked two jobs to make it through college, he rarely joined them.

When Al graduated, he got a nice job with LoonaTechnologies, an East Coast conglomerate that developed communications systems for NASA's moon landings. LoonaTech now sold all manner of communications devices—telephones and cell phones, pagers, walkie-talkies, and intercom systems. The regular schedule of a single full-time job at least allowed Al to join his pals every weekend on the boardwalk. Trouble was, his circle of friends was quickly diminishing as his buddies succumbed to the tug of domestic life or lucrative job opportunities somewhere else. It wasn't long before Al was the last of the boardwalk regulars practicing the sacred ritual of a boardwalk weekend.

Just what was a boardwalk weekend? It was Friday night barhopping to the tune of fifty-cent beers and dollar shots (vomiting or passing out before sunrise was frowned upon). It was sleeping most of Saturday on the sand of a sunlit beach, the sounds of the ocean waves creating the ultimate Valium. It was early cocktails and a seafood dinner followed by a night of dancing and singing with local bands, each one piercing the salty air with blazing riffs that echoed up and down the coast. It was enjoying the poets, belly dancers, folksingers, odd talents, and drifters who entertained along the boardwalk until dawn just for the toss of a few coins from passersby. It was sleeping until noon on Sunday followed by a brunch at one of the local hotels. Finally, as Sunday evening approached, it was realizing that the fun was over and contemplating how to survive another week until Friday night came again.

It was during one of his solo barhops, twenty years ago, that Al met Liz Buckman, herself a self-styled bohemian queen of the boardwalk weekend. She was the forever-tanned blonde on the posters and commercials enticing visitors to the beach. Liz loved to sing and dance with the Saturday night bands. Al had seen her a few times before, but on one particular night, he bought her a drink and they danced. He admired her face—classic and round, features softly sculpted, her eyes a hypnotic hazel, as Al came to call them. She smiled with the best of the beach beauties, but it was her let-it-all-loose laugh that closed the sale for Al. He admired her graceful and fluid motion, and he admired her ability to have a good time. In fact, Liz glided through life with few cares and fewer worries. She had no particular ambition—having never held a job longer than six months—but she respected ambition in others and it looked like Al had more than enough for the both of them. Partial to large sun hats and colorful saris, Liz herself was an attraction on any boardwalk weekend.

Al and Liz came to look forward to their time together on weekends and soon began seeing each other more frequently. After a courtship that Al managed to squeeze between business trips, they married, but Al's heart remained entwined in his career at LoonaTech. Al gave up boardwalk weekends as his dedication and ever-present work ethic took him to a vice presidency after fifteen years at LoonaTech. Liz continued visiting the boardwalk solo for a while, but there wasn't much a married, encroaching-on-middle-age housewife could do for fun alone down there. She complained for years—but didn't every wife? Only after some time in marriage counseling did Al realize theirs was a broken union, and by the time he turned his attention more fully to his wife, she had long ago turned her attention to someone else, somewhere else.

The divorce broke Al's stride, if not his heart. Much as he loved Liz in his way, his inner turmoil was as much about failing as it was about lost love. Al hated failing at anything, and this divorce was a failure he could not come to terms with.

He lost his footing at LoonaTechnologies. His boss, Richard Lynn, a decent guy and a good friend, helped cover for Al in his difficult times, but a year ago a new management team came in and things changed for the worse. During their years climbing the corporate ladder together, Richard constantly reminded Al that their careers were just one incompetent moron away from coming to an abrupt end. That moron showed up on this new management team and unsympathetically swept Al, Richard, and many of Al's colleagues to the unemployment line. After twenty years, there were no more projects, no more meetings, no more higher-level butts to kiss. Al was suddenly on the outside looking in—no thank you . . . no gold watch . . . no job.

Al maintained the veneer. None of these setbacks was going to do him in. He always looked the part—confident, wise, patrician. He was almost always the tallest guy in the room, with thinning wavy hair swirling with gray, and a pair of unnervingly blue eyes that made people think he was more intense than he really was. He was only a few pounds overweight, but his stooping shoulders made him look heavier. He remained a good writer and a raconteur, but those talents were known only to an exceedingly small circle of friends.

When you summed it all up, despite his veneer, his talents, and his playing by the rules, Al had nothing to show for his forty-five years. He was divorced, childless, and unemployed.

And, to top it off, he had only a few more hours to live.

CHAPTER 2

maxie's tavern

MAXIE'S TAVERN WAS the watering hole for workers from LoonaTech. Dick and Al started the tradition. Everybody would button down all week at the office, then roll-up their sleeves and loosen their ties for a Friday night blowout at Maxie's. With board-walk weekends a thing of the past, these Friday nights had become a tradition that Al looked forward to more than most anything in his life. Being gone from LoonaTech this past year didn't dampen his enthusiasm. He still showed up for the Friday night shindig, and too bad if that made some of the new employees uncomfortable.

Maxie's Tavern was a rustic tavern at the north end of the Seafarer Beach and Boardwalk. Seafarer Beach was north of the more popular Jersey resorts, wedged in an inlet between the Jersey coast and a series of offshore jetties.

Because this kept the ocean waves calm, Seafarer attracted what you might call an older clientele. In fact, regulars to the Jersey Shore said that Seafarer sold more Ex-Lax than suntan lotion on any given summer's day, that defibrillators were a hotter buy than surfboards, and that instead of toxic waste occasionally washing up on shore, beach walkers would occasionally find a set of teeth or an empty bottle of Viagra.

The boardwalk at Seafarer Beach was an old-fashioned amusement pier. Supported by pylons driven deep beneath the sand by New Deal workers in the early 1930s, the boardwalk was a raised platform of two-by-fours that loomed about twelve feet above and stretched the length of the beach. It offered the usual array of restaurants, shops, games of chance, traditional rides, and offbeat attractions. A separate portion of the boardwalk jutted out over the ocean and offered the more modern thrill rides, many of which were designed to make riders feel as if they were flying over the open water. Al always figured they designed it this way so people would throw up right into the ocean instead of on the pier.

Maxie's anchored the northern end of the boardwalk, right next to the shooting gallery. Low ceilings, bay windows overlooking the ocean, salty old bartenders, and the smell of fried seafood were the coin of the realm at Maxie's. Nothing ever changed; not even the air, which still had the blue-tinged smell of nicotine to it despite a smoking ban instituted five years ago.

You would see the same tables, the same bric-a-brac, and the same menu today as you would on the day Maxie's opened in 1947.

Time stood still at Maxie's. And so did the waitresses.

℃ "Can we get another pitcher of beer over here?" shouted Paul Gergen over the din of the patrons and the numbing music of the jukebox.

"You go get it!" Sandy Trent shouted back, pushing the empty pitchers in front of Gergen. "I don't think the waitresses are coming back for a while."

Looking over at the bar, Paul and Sandy could see two of the waitresses doing a series of shots at the bar with customers and the third climbing on the bar to dance.

"Be damned if I'm going to leave them a tip," Gergen mumbled, grabbing the pitchers and staggering toward the bar.

"Alert the state budget director!" Sandy shouted to no one in particular. "Gergen's holding back on his tips again! Tax revenue to plummet!" Sandy giggled her inebriated little giggle, then turned her attention to Al, who was sitting forlornly between two empty chairs. Sandy and Paul were the only ones at the table with whom Al had worked at LoonaTech. Everyone else was a disciple of LoonaTech's new management team, and although they came to Maxie's for the Friday fling, they kept to themselves.

Gergen returned with two pitchers held unevenly in his hands, beer streaming down the sides of both. He began filling everyone's glass in one continuous pour, not the least bit worried about how much beer he was spilling on the table. The spilling beer jogged Al's memory to LoonaTech's Christmas party at Maxie's some years ago.

December 1995

Liz began laughing hysterically at whatever Dick Lynn had just said to her. It was not lost on Al that Liz seemed to have an easier time laughing with Dick than with him . . . or that she was practically sitting in his lap.

"What did he say to you?" Al asked Liz.

"Some old joke," she replied.

"Can't you share it with me? I like a good joke, too."

"You used to . . ." Liz said sadly. "Not any more."

"I still like a good laugh," Al said defensively, but decided it wasn't worth another argument. "Oh, forget it."

"I'll tell you," Liz said. "Horse goes into a bar. Bartender says, 'Hey, why the long face?'" She began giggling uncontrollably.

"You think that's funny?" Al asked.

"Yes! It's the way he says it that's so funny." She stopped giggling for a moment. "At least Dick Lynn tries to be funny," Liz said to Al coldly. She started laughing again and grabbed the almost-overflowing pitcher of beer and began pouring it into the glasses without regard for how much she was spilling on the table. The beer was forming its own river along the table's edge and dripping off the far end. The more everyone around the table yelled at Liz to be careful, the harder she laughed and the more beer she spilled.

Dick dropped to his knees and twisted his face upward, letting the river of beer drip from the table directly into his mouth. After a chorus of objections about how gross that was, Dick straightened up and tried to wrest the pitcher from Liz's grasp. She quickly swung her hand at the beer cascading out of the pitcher and splashed it in Dick's face. Without thinking, Dick picked up his half-filled glass and flung its contents right into Liz's face. Soon everyone was giving everyone else a beer bath.

It seemed to Al he could still smell the beer on his clothes just as clearly as he could that night a decade ago. He realized it had been a year since his last contact with her. He wondered where Liz was now—did she still live in the state . . . did she find someone else . . . how happy was she? Suddenly, he felt Sandy jabbing at his elbow.

"Earth to Al . . . earth to Al," Sandy shouted, "anything new on the job front?"

Al snapped out of his thoughts.

"Kazakhstan is looking for a new president." He shrugged.

"Sounds promising." Sandy grabbed the glass from Al's hand and finished the beer in it. "What qualifications do you need to be president of Kazakhstan?"

"First, you have to be able to spell it."

"That leaves me out." Sandy gave him back his glass. "I can't even say it."

"Second, you have to know how to tend goats. That's where I might run into some trouble." Al leaned over, a bit tipsy, and whispered in Sandy's ear. "I hear they let goats vote in Kazakhstan. I'll never carry the goat vote." Al exaggerated a frown of disappointment.

"Can you blame the goats, considering how many you defiled here in the U.S.?" Sandy bellowed her reply, causing a few quizzical looks from the others at the table. "Did you ever consider Burkina Faso?" she asked.

"Burkin what?"

"Burkina Faso."

"Is that a skin disease or something?"

"It's a country in western Africa. I read in the *New York Times* today that they need a minister of defense."

"Defense against what?" Al wondered.

"Maybe an invasion of goats from Kazakhstan," Sandy replied.

"Why would I want to be defense minister of Burkina Fatso after I've been vice president of marketing at LoonaTechnologies?" Al harrumphed playfully. "What a humiliating step down that would be!"

"I take it from this nonsensical conversation that you have no job prospects?" Sandy said sympathetically.

"None whatsoever," Al said flatly.

CHAPTER 3

the young turks

SANDY EXCUSED HERSELF to the ladies' room. Al watched her walk away, then turned his attention to the new legion of LoonaTech management sitting at the other end of the table. A few weeks ago, Sandy had told him that around the office they were called the young turks.

"More like young jerks," Al had replied.

They huddled tightly together, their comments and conversation limited only to themselves. He studied them with a bit of envy—after all, most of them were just starting their careers—and a large dose of contempt. As far as Al was concerned, they were arrogant little cusses who did nothing more than inherit everything

Al, Dick Lynn, and Al's colleagues had built at the company, and who then proceeded to ruin it with scatterbrained and inexperienced ideas.

The leader of the turks was a plump lady in her mid-thirties. Her name was Hope Himmelmann and, ironically, she was the only one of the group who had been with LoonaTech for many years. She was frumpy on her good days, out-and-out unkempt the rest of the time. She had an annoyingly vacant smile, which Al thought accurately reflected the amount of brainpower she exhibited on the job. Even the normally chivalrous and ever-tolerant Richard Lynn called her "Hope-less."

Hope Himmelmann had jumped from job to job at LoonaTech, staying at each position until her boss realized she contributed nothing of value. Because the rules for firing employees were strict and convoluted, and a large company like LoonaTech was always open to lawsuits from employees who were fired, supervisors were more apt to transfer unproductive employees to other groups within the company rather than fire them. That is how Hope survived at LoonaTech for over ten years, proving the maxim that it is harder to hit a moving target.

When the new management came along last year, Hope immediately latched onto them and they onto her because she demonstrated an unmatched ability to tell them exactly what they wanted to hear. The new management was forcing changes that existing managers like Al and Dick Lynn thought were wrong, but Hope fell right into line and she quickly found herself in a position of prominence. Now she sat amidst the young turks like a waddling Buddha accepting worshipful stares from her minions.

"How are you, Hope?" Al shouted across the table.

"Very well," she smirked back, barely a hint of sincerity in her reply. "Since we instituted the Executive Decision-Making Matrix in January, we've been going great."

Al bit his lip at the mention of the matrix. It was not an accident that she mentioned it. Everyone at LoonaTech knew that Al's run-in with the creator of the matrix was the beginning of the end of his career. And it so happened that the creator of the matrix, Samuel Venable, a Harvard MBA–type who graduated the year before last, was sitting right next to Hope, firmly clutching a bottle of spring water. Venable nodded impassively at Al.

Two Years Ago

    Venable swept into Al's office with a quick afterthought of a knock on the door. Al looked up from a report he was reading as Venable planted himself in a chair directly across from Al. A number of people at the company had complained that Venable, like many of the new managers, was arrogant and without manners— something Al found very annoying.

    "You have a minute?" Venable asked.

    "It would be pretty embarrassing for you if I didn't," *Al replied, "since you're already in here, Sam."*

    "Samuel," Venable corrected him. "I go by Samuel. This will only take a minute."

    "What can I do for you?" Al asked warily.

    "I have developed this evaluation tool." Venable handed Al a thick bound document that Al could barely hold in one hand. "This is a series of questions and

tests we are going to give all our managers."

"What for?" Al asked.

"We want to evaluate their decision-making capabilities, since, after all, judgment and decision-making is what we pay our executives for, isn't it?"

"Sometimes I wonder." Al laughed but got nothing in response from Venable but a frown. Al weighed the document in his hand. "You sure this is to test our decision-making and not our muscles?"

"It's only as big as it is because it's the most comprehensive survey of its kind," Venable said proudly. "Mr. Erie wants me to talk to you about what to call the study." Venable was referring to John G. Erie, the new chief marketing officer who had brought in this new stable of people.

"Okay." Al thought a moment. "How about 'The Survey to Evaluate Executive Decision-Making'?" Al handed the document back to Venable, who looked obviously displeased with the suggestion.

"That doesn't really say anything," Venable said. "It doesn't convey the weight of what this survey is."

"The only thing that could convey the weight of that survey is an eighteen-wheeler," Al said, slightly annoyed.

"I think we should give it a different name," Venable said.

"How about Ralph?" Al said.

Venable ignored Al's joke.

"I was thinking of calling it 'The Attitudinal and

Evaluative Parameter Matrix for the Measurement of Existing and Newly Established Paradigms in Thought-Process and Decision-Making Effectiveness.'"

Al thought for a moment. "Oh. If you wanted something simple and direct, why didn't you say so?" he said sarcastically.

"Then you support my idea for the name?" Venable stood up.

"Actually, I liked my suggestion better." Al smiled. Venable looked at him as though he were Benedict Arnold.

"You can't keep to the old ways of thinking and doing things," Venable said as he sprang from the chair. "Change is the lifeblood of any organization, Mr. Mitchell."

Al angrily slapped his pen down on the desk.

"That what your vast experience in the workplace tells you?" Al maintained his sarcastic tone. "All ten months of it?"

Venable, his hand on the doorknob, stopped and turned around but decided to hold his tongue.

"Thanks for your time," he monotoned.

"Thanks for coming by, Sam," Al responded. "Do me a favor. Next time check with my secretary first before you come barging in here."

Venable studied Al for a moment.

"It's Samuel." Venable said coldly.

"Oh, yes. Thanks for reminding me." Al stared back, just as coldly. Venable turned and left the room.

Al knew Venable would dutifully report his cavalier
attitude to the new chief marketing officer. Al knew
he had painted a big red bull's-eye on his back and
it wouldn't be long before John G. Erie had him in
the crosshairs.

"You going to join us?" Gergen shouted to the daydreaming Al.

Al hadn't noticed that Sandy had returned to the table and that they were proposing a toast. "Here's to the old guard," he said wistfully.

"Here's to us." Sandy raised her glass.

"Here's to not working at LoonaTechnologies anymore," Al said loud enough for the rest of the table to hear.

"Shush! Keep your voice down," Sandy admonished him. "Someday you might want to come back. . . ."

"I'll be dogcatcher in Burkina Fatso before I ever work at LoonaTechnologies, as long as that snake of a chief marketing officer is still there."

Sandy whacked Al on the arm. "Stop it!" she pleaded.

"He's a jerk. In fact . . ." Al thought for a moment, then said loudly, "he is the biggest jerk I ever met in my life. And, believe me, there have been more than a few jerks in my life!" The young turks did not let on whether they heard Al's toast or had any reaction to it.

"Be careful what you say!" Sandy jabbed Al's arm.

"Why? He can't do anything else to me."

"He can do something to me!" Sandy said, suddenly serious. "I still have to work there." That thought hadn't registered with Al.

"Sorry," he said softly to her, then raised his voice again for all to hear.

"Your attention, please, ladies and gentlemen, the opinions expressed by yours truly are mine and mine only. They do not represent and should be construed to represent the opinions of Maxie's management, Seafarer Beach, or anyone at this table, living or dead. Thank you."

"That ought to do it," Sandy deadpanned.

"I'm going to take a little walk," Al said. "Gonna get me some fresh air."

"You want me to go with you?" Sandy asked.

"Nah, stay here and finish the round for me. I should be back for the next one."

Al squeezed through the wall-to-wall revelers and pushed his way out the door and onto the boardwalk. He took a couple of long, deep breaths. Nothing like crisp sea air to convince Al he was feeling better than he thought.

"Yo, Al," called a familiar voice from behind.

"Dick!" Al shouted before even turning. He beamed, holding his hand out happily. "You made it!" Al was genuinely pleased to see his friend. Dick Lynn, already past fifty, sported an almost uncontrollable waft of blond hair, a thick mustache, and the early etchings of a beard. He was overweight, and he knew it. He just didn't care. To Dick, a few extra good meals was worth scratching off some years at the tail end of his life.

"Sure, I made it." Dick smiled, shaking Al's hand. "I got nothing else to do. Where are you going?"

"Just getting some air for a minute—Sandy and Paul are inside at the usual table."

"They by themselves?" Dick asked.

"No. Hope and some of her storm troopers are there. Don't

worry, though. It's casual-dress Friday. They left the jackboots and the armbands at home."

"By the way"—Dick beamed—"I got a line on a job opening at Eastern Wireless Communications. It would be perfect for you."

"Thanks—" Al began to say, then caught himself. "Why are you telling me about this job? Why aren't you going after it yourself?"

Dick shrugged and smiled weakly. "Let's talk about it when you come back."

"You still feel guilty for firing me, don't you?" Al asked. "How many times I got to say it? It wasn't your fault. Could you help it if our esteemed chief marketing officer didn't have balls enough to tell me himself that I was fired?" Al opened the door to Maxie's for Dick. "Go have a drink. I'll be back in a few minutes."

"Okay." Dick patted Al on the shoulder and slipped into Maxie's. He quickly squeezed through the crowd of patrons and found the table and greeted Paul and Sandy. He gave the young turks a silent and polite nod.

"Anything new on the job front?" Sandy asked Dick.

Dick shrugged. "Why? You hear of something?"

"I hear Kazakhstan is looking for a new president," Sandy said.

CHAPTER 4

wheel of miss fortune

*T*IME AND PROGRESS had changed most everything at the boardwalk. The guns in the shooting gallery used laser beams instead of corks. The pinball machines were 3-D and the video games were now virtual reality. There was no greater misnomer than "penny arcade."

Sitting in front of the arched entranceway to the arcade was one stable and unchanged attraction—probably the oldest on the boardwalk. Originally called the Gypsy Sisters when it debuted in 1932, it was now known as the Wheel of Fortune-Tellers.

Encased in a clear plastic bubble were two mannequins, the one on the left a young angelic-looking girl in a silky white and yellow dress. She was called Lady Luck. It was said she always brought good fortune. Her counterpart in the other half of the bubble was a Margaret-Hamilton-Wicked-Witch-of-the-West-type called Miss Fortune. She wore a black robe trimmed in purple, sat in a dim twilight, and was obviously the habitual bearer of bad tidings.

In the center of the bubble was a spinning wheel, the left half on Lady Luck's side, the other half on Miss Fortune's. A thick black line clearly delineated the two sides of the wheel. When a quarter went into the coin drop, the needle on the wheel would spin, and whichever half of the wheel it pointed to when it stopped, that mannequin would be activated to tell the customer's fortune. The wheel was supposed to be random, but in all the years Al watched or used the machine, he had never seen the needle stop on Miss Fortune's side of the wheel. Al determined the powers-that-be fixed the wheel—*programmed* might be the gentler word—so that it always stopped on Lady Luck, because they were afraid too many people would be spooked by getting bad news from Miss Fortune.

Al had always been attracted to the older, unchanged items on the boardwalk and he rarely ever failed to stop for a conversation with Lady Luck. He pushed his quarter into the coin drop and the needle on the wheel began to spin. Al rooted, as he always did, for the needle to point to Miss Fortune, so that just once he could find out what she had to say. The needle swirled around a few times, then began to slow. Its momentum barely carried it to the top of the wheel one more time, and as it came to a stop, it just barely edged onto Miss Fortune's side. Before Al could register his surprise, the darkened half of the bubble brightened, as did Miss Fortune's animatronic face and eyes. A sinister, if somewhat tinny, laugh bellowed out of the loudspeaker.

"Hello, dearie," she cackled, rubbing her waxen hands together with glee. "So . . . you want to visit me instead of my goody-two-shoes sister?" she cackled, pointing with a bent right finger at Lady Luck. "You think you are brave enough to deal with me?" she asked. "I warn you! Dealing with me is like nothing you have ever experienced before."

Al chuckled. "Honey, last time I heard that from a girl, I wound up marrying her," he said to the mannequin. Miss Fortune waved her hands dramatically in front of her.

"You still want me to tell you your fortune, eh?" she continued. "All right . . . but I should warn you, I'm not the nicest person in the world. In fact, some people think I'm an out-and-out bit—, I mean, witch." She began laughing hysterically.

"Sounds like you should be working at LoonaTechnologies," Al said back to the mechanical face.

"Let me look at you," Miss Fortune continued, "and I will tell you what you want to know." Her eyes seemed to truly fix on him. "Not much to look at, are you, dearie? I thought the geek-fest was next week!" Miss Fortune's body twisted and turned in fine animatronic laughter. Finally, she stopped and stared silently at Al for a few seconds before saying, "Miss Fortune has visited you."

As she spoke, she pointed downward and a card popped out of a slot next to the coin drop. Miss Fortune offered one last cackle and returned to her original lifeless pose. Al stooped to pick up the card, all the while staring at Miss Fortune's darkened eyes. They seemed to follow his movements with a precision that unnerved

Al for a quick moment. As he pulled the card from the slot, Miss Fortune suddenly lit up again.

"It is a misfortune that you didn't take this seriously," she said quietly, gravely, then darkened into lifelessness again. Al was startled. Lady Luck never came to life a second time like that.

"Must have reprogrammed you," he said, frowning at the darkened figure, and then turned his attention to the fortune card:

Prepare for the ride of your life.

"Hey!" Al thought. "That's something else my wife promised me." But he had no idea what it meant in this context.

Al flipped the card to see if there was anything to read on the other side. It was blank. He was hugely disappointed. Normally, the cards from Lady Luck gave him two or three cleverly rhyming verses for his quarter. He stuffed the card into his shirt pocket and continued down the boardwalk. He had one more stop to make. Ahead lay the memories of his youth and a rendezvous with the end of his life.

CHAPTER 5

the roundabout

COMPLETELY FORGETTING ABOUT the fortune card, Al moved quickly down the boardwalk, watching people enjoy everything it had to offer—hot dogs, hamburgers, steak sandwiches, Chinese food, Greek barbecue, fresh-catch-of-the-day seafood, pizza, baked potatoes with anything on them, lobster, oysters, clams on the half shell, corn on the cob, pretzels, funnel cakes, ice cream, banana splits, shakes, and flavored ice. Yes, the boardwalk had everything except thin people.

Al continued past the thrill rides with complete disinterest. There was only one ride for him. They might build a roller coaster as fast as a bullet or as high as the clouds—but nothing would ever compare to the Roundabout.

The Roundabout was the first attraction ever built at Seafarer. It was a traditional merry-go-round and it opened in the summer of 1932. It remained a top attraction through many generations, until the Psychedelic Sixties, when kids condemned anything their parents enjoyed as "square" and something as traditional as a merry-go-round as a tool of the "establishment." Besides, a ten-mile-an-hour ride on a mechanical horse didn't stand much of a chance against the sex, drug, and rock-and-roll revolution. The ride was shut down in the early 1970s and condemned a few years later. For a while, Seafarer Beach was happy to let it stand as a rubble-strewn reminder of a quaint earlier time, but when discussion to demolish it really got serious in the 1980s, along came a local businessman-turned-multimillionaire bond trader.

Capitalizing on the nostalgia trend of that decade, the multi-millionaire bought the Roundabout and financed a complete restoration until it was the envy of every amusement pier and theme park up and down the eastern seaboard. No expense was spared in resuscitating its former glory, from the gold-encrusted ornamental decorations along its canopy, to the immaculate wood flooring on its deck. Most striking were the lovingly painted hand-crafted horses in their many colors, many poses.

A new enclosed room was built for the Roundabout to protect it from the elements and the corrosive sea air. The intimate circular room re-created the feel of the Victorian era, with wall murals showing beach bathers at the turn of the nineteenth century and elaborately designed wooden benches and high-backed chairs scattered around the room. There were brightly colored bubble gum machines and a nickelodeon. There was also a three-foot-high barrier encircling the Roundabout, acting as a perimeter to prevent people from hopping on the ride while it was in motion. The barrier was designed and painted to look like a white picket fence. Completing the room was a ticket booth at the entrance and a newsstand along the back wall, where two men in period garb sold newspapers, candy, and best-selling books.

Al walked in and stepped up to the ticket booth. The bored girl took his money and ripped off a ticket, which she gently tossed at him. Al ignored the queer look she gave him for wanting to ride the merry-go-round solo. He was certain she hadn't the faintest notion of the heritage she was helping to preserve. Al took his place in line behind a pair of young teenaged daters and immediately fixed his gaze on his favorite horse, a mare painted black from head to hoof, its front legs pumped high as if it were running the Clubhouse Turn at Churchill Downs.

Memories came rushing back. It was here that Al brought Liz Buckman on the night of their first date. After a few Friday nights of "spontaneously" meeting at Maxie's, he had finally asked her on a date, and after a dinner at the locals' favorite seafood place, Attack of the Crab Shack, Al brought Liz here and he confided in her his fascination for his favorite horse, which he called Night, for its unrelenting blackness.

May 1985

> *"See the mare over there?" Al pointed. "The all-black one? She's my buddy. I call her Night." He plunked Liz with his elbow playfully. "Get it? Night-mare."*
>
> *"I got it. Very clever," she shouted in his ear to overcome the loud organ music. "You have a talent*

with words. I'm not sure what that talent is, but . . ."
They both laughed as they took their position behind
the barrier.

"You surprised me." Liz patted him on the shoulder.
"I figured you for a roller-coaster kind of guy."

"Really?" Al was surprised. "Why?"

"I don't know. . . . you seem like a high-energy
person. I think you like to have life happen quickly.
You like the thrill of unexpected turns . . . of living on
the edge. Am I right?"

"That depends on what you think a merry-go-round
kind of guy is."

Liz thought for a moment. "Maybe somebody who
honors life's traditions . . . someone who takes life more
deliberately . . . plans everything out before he acts . . .
like an engineer or an architect."

"Just for the record, I like coasters fine," Al said,
hedging his bet in case Liz was a big roller-coaster fan.
"But I like this ride, too. I like the fact it's relaxing. It's
nostalgic. It speaks of another time . . . what must have
been a better time. So I guess I'm a deliberate kind of
guy who honors life's traditions, but who likes life to
happen quickly, and who enjoys a few twists and turns.
What about you? Are you a roller-coaster kind of girl?"

"God, no," Liz responded. "I get dizzy on a scooter.
I don't like being on things that go too fast."

"That's funny," Al said. "I wouldn't have taken you
for a slowpoke."

"I'm not. I'm a chicken."

They laughed as the bell clanged twice, signaling the end of the ride.

"When they let us on, go right for Night," Al told her. "There is a gray filly right next to her that would be perfect for you."

"I'll try and keep up." Liz smiled.

When everyone had cleared the ride and they opened the perimeter gate, Al made his way over to his favorite horse with Liz in tow. He helped her mount the filly, then jumped on Night. The bell clanged once, signaling the start of the ride.

As they went around and around, Al would point out the unique and humorous sights of the mural portraits on the wall. Liz listened attentively and laughed the laugh of a girl who wants her man to know how funny she thinks he is.

As the ride came to a stop, Al slipped off Night and helped Liz down off her horse. The remaining momentum of the ride pushed her into him and they enjoyed their first prolonged kiss.

Since then, Al made it a point to take a spin on his favorite horse once every Friday night, no matter how unhappy the memories. In fact, Al would tell you that any ride that went around in circles and ended up right where it started was a perfect metaphor for his life.

The bell clanged once. The ride was about to board. The gate opened and Al made his way directly to Night and hopped on. He handed his ticket to another attendant, this one a long-haired, open-shirted teenager who walked around the ride admonishing everyone in a barely audible mumble to put on and tighten the seat belts attached to the horses.

The clock on the wall in the Roundabout room read exactly eight o'clock when the clang of the bell signaled the start of the ride and it spun to life.

In its early days, a manual operator controlled a lever and brake system to start and stop the Roundabout. Now, it was done by computer. Trouble was, the computer software managing this ride had within its almost-infinite lines of programming code a cyber-glitch so subtle it was undetectable to human senses—undetectable, that is, until it manifested itself as a problem, which it was about to do.

The first few turns were fine. Al began to relax, closing his eyes and pretending Liz was laughing on the gray filly next to him.

By the fourth turn, however, something felt wrong. Al felt a bit dizzy. He opened his eyes. The ride was turning faster than he'd ever experienced before, fast enough that he had to wrap both his arms around the pole that secured Night to the canopy and the floor of the merry-go-round.

As he passed by, Al watched the long-haired attendant in the control booth frantically looking at the controls.

Screams were emanating from behind Al as the ride continued to pick up speed.

Al leaned more on the support pole to keep from being thrown off. What he could not see as he did this was the stress fractures—ever so slight, but beginning to widen—where Night's support pole was anchored to the canopy of the ride. Finally, after an interminable few more turns, the clanging bell was heard again and a voice came over the loudspeaker urging everyone on the ride to remain calm.

The teenaged attendant jumped on the merry-go-round and made his way to the room at the center, where the gears that drove the ride continued to turn out of control. The attendant leaned forward to look at a set of gears and never saw his car keys fall out of his pocket. The keys fell and wedged themselves between the two biggest gears, bringing them to a grinding, groaning halt. The Roundabout itself also came to a sudden stop. Unfortunately, Night didn't.

Strained by Al's weight and the hard stop, Night's support pole snapped from its moorings and, like an acrylic, wingless Pegasus, Night flew off the ride with Al still holding on. Just then, the controller's voice came on reassuringly to tell everyone, "We have applied emergency measures to stop the ride. You may feel a jerking motion as the ride comes to a stop."

The controller's voice came on again. "Please hold on to your horse until it has achieved a complete stop."

By this point, Night had cleared the ride itself and reached the wooden barrier. Its front hoofs hit the top of the barrier, upending the horse, and flinging Al in the air ahead of it. As Al flew off the horse, a picture of Miss Fortune's card flashed through his mind:

Prepare for the ride of your life.

Al closed his eyes and braced himself. He hit the floor and took the force of the concussion on the left side of his head. He could feel the friction burns eating at his knees and elbows, when suddenly a skull-splitting headache disoriented him. A few seconds later, he crashed into the front of the newsstand, with Night's butt crashing in behind him. The force of the collision upended a book display directly above them both. Dozens of copies of *Tuesdays with Morrie* by Mitch Albom came raining down on them.

For a few moments, Al heard nothing, felt nothing. Then, as his head exploded in pain, he heard a blast of static from a walkie-talkie and an unfamiliar voice.

"Horse 245 has jumped the stall and we have a man down!"

A second burst of static followed. It was the last thing Al ever heard.

life flashes

*I*T'S TRUE WHAT they say about your life flashing in front of you in those last moments. Considering Al's life, that wasn't such a good thing. Most people had life flashes focused on a warm embrace, a happy wedding day, a walk in the park, opening presents on a festive Christmas morning.

Not Al.

The static from the walkie-talkie faded. Al felt a little wobbly and unsure of himself. His memory was replaying the last visuals he had seen on earth. Flying off the Roundabout, there was the skinny man with the handlebar mustache and the proper lady in the horizontally striped two-piece bathing suit waving to him from the wall mural. There was the clerk in the newsstand throwing his arms up to protect himself as Al and Night came bulleting in. And finally, fittingly, the very last thing Al saw as he lay on the ground—Night's huge black butt skidding right toward his head.

Al's eyelids fluttered open. His head was surprisingly clear; the pain had faded completely. Surrounded by a swirling white mist, Al could not tell if he was sitting, standing, moving, or still. The mist swirled into the outline of a human form, which began to flesh itself into a familiar, if not welcome, figure from Al's youth.

It was Mrs. Turtletaub, Al's unflinching and relentless third-grade teacher, her silver hair in a bouffant style like Jackie Kennedy's, her eyes peering through a pair of pointy, thick-framed eyeglasses popular in the 1960s. There she was, standing over Al, frighteningly real, holding an incredibly thick math textbook. She was admonishing him for his lack of expertise in multiplication.

"Do your eight times table!" she demanded. Her arms suddenly snapped out, cobralike, and reached for Al's ears. Pulling students up out of their chairs by their ears was one of Mrs. Turtletaub's favorite maneuvers. Remembering this, Al threw his hands up over his head, but he wasn't fast enough. He felt her hand twist and pull on his right ear. Strangely, while it was annoying to him, it did not hurt at all.

"Stand up, young man!" she barked. "Are you telling me you cannot do your times table?" Without waiting for a reply, Mrs. Turtletaub's face wrinkled with disdain. "This is unacceptable, young man. If you can't multiply, you will never add up to anything!" She laughed at her own pun and then turned deadly serious once again.

"I want you to write your eight times tables for me one hundred times tonight!" She let go of Al's ear and stood there imperiously; arms folded, with a stare that could melt Everest.

Al tried to blink her away. Slowly, she began to dissolve, until her outline was one with the mist. It began to re-form into the shape of another person, this one of elephantine proportions. What was once the hard, unforgiving face of Mrs. Turtletaub stretched and compressed into the sad-eyed doughy face of Ray Pomeroy, a former colleague of Al's early career, a poor wretch of a man whose insatiable appetite had him tipping the scales at 350 or more pounds. Self-loathing because of his weight, Pomeroy was not the jolly type. He was an argument waiting to happen—with anybody about anything—right up until his heart gave out on his thirty-fourth birthday.

"You think I didn't hear you guys making fun of me all those years?" Pomeroy growled at Al. 'Hey, guys!' he shouted, as though imitating Al. 'What is Pomeroy going to do this summer? Sell shade at the beach! Hey, guys! What happened when Pomeroy fell asleep on the beach? People hosed him down until Greenpeace got there! Hey, guys, what will Pomeroy do in the hot weather? Smell!' You think I didn't hear all that?" Pomeroy began calling Al every name in the book. He droned on until his voice meshed with a high-pitched buzz that, at first, sounded like a buzzing insect, then became more distinct and identifiable as the high-pitched whirr of a dentist's drill.

"Just sit back and relax," said the melodic, resonant voice. "Everything will be all right." Pomeroy was gone and a new figure was sculpted out of the mist. Standing directly over Al was Dr. John Hammer, Al's boyhood dentist. Known as Jack to his patients, he was best remembered for specializing in dental practices perfected during the Middle Ages. It was rumored Hammer learned his techniques from watching Laurence Olivier in *Marathon Man*.

A burly onetime college football linebacker who constantly bragged to his patients that he played the state championship football game with a broken bone in his leg, Dr. Jack wasn't big on babying patients or providing them incidentals like Novocain. Hammer once gave Al a root canal without using any painkiller, saying pain was good for the soul. By the time that root canal was over, Al figured he had enough soul to own Motown Records.

Now Dr. Jack was hovering over Al, moving in, his tree-limb forearms preparing to do his brutish work.

"Should we see if we can give the tooth fairy some business?" Hammer asked brightly, producing a pair of long-nosed steel pliers and dangling them distressingly close to Al's mouth. Al began violently turning his head and he wrenched his jaw and eyes tightly shut.

"Come on now, don't give me a hard time." Hammer grabbed Al's jaw with his free hand, laughing convivially, as if this were a party. Al could feel the dentist's powerful hands, and just as his jaw muscles were giving way, the grip was loosened and Hammer's deep, throaty guffaws became a nasal donkey-bray of a laugh that, once he recognized it, made Al's skin crawl.

Al tried to persuade himself that it couldn't be real . . . of all the relatives to meet at the end of his life. Al slowly opened one eye. . . . Sure enough, there stood his little dweeb of a brother-in-law, Stanley Dormfner, bald, sniveling, snickering; a nails-scratching-the-chalkboard kind of guy; a disaster of a financial planner who twenty years ago advised Al not to invest in CDs—"a passing phase, that's all." For that matter, he called Microsoft a "fly-by-night operation" that nobody would remember in ten years and laughed off an investment in Starbucks because "nobody but nobody is going to pay five dollars for a cup of coffee!"

Suddenly Al had a wrenching thought. There was no way that Stanley Dormfner would be in his vision of heaven, and Al did die suddenly, unexpectedly, before a priest could administer final absolution. . . . *What if this was hell?* Was it possible? Al raced through the many vices he had indulged in on earth and the sins he could remember committing. "No worse than anybody else," he thought. Given the price he was about to pay, he hoped they had all been worthwhile.

"So, what did you leave your family, Al?" Stanley whined. "Nothing, right? What did I tell you about investing in the tax-free munis when they were a good deal? And what about the 401(k)? Didn't I tell you that you'd be sorry for not jumping on my advice? Didn't I? Didn't I?" He raised his whine to an unbearable pitch. *"Well, didn't I?"*

Something about Stanley's ultra-irritating ways suddenly assuaged Al's concerns. He reassured himself that this couldn't be hell—Satan might be evil, but he wasn't a masochist. If Stanley Dormfner had appeared at hell's gate, Satan would have closed the place down for all time. This had to be someplace else.

Now the swirling mist enveloped Stanley and he disappeared from view and so did the mist. A white light, warm and soothing, eased over Al's face and body, giving him an immediate feeling of peace. Not only did his head no longer hurt, but the friction burns on his elbows and knees became fiction burns—disappearing altogether. Suddenly Al Mitchell felt very good . . . better than he had felt in such a long time. It felt a bit strange to feel so good.

"Hello, Mr. Mitchell," a soft voice called out. Al turned. A diminutive boylike cherub floated happily in the air next to him. "Seeing those people must have been a bummer," the cherub said, "especially that fat guy." Al nodded in agreement. "You know, Mr. Mitchell, you have to start thinking more positive things. If you thought happier thoughts, the results would be a lot better for you!" The boy squinted hard, as if studying every inch of Al's physical appearance. "Not big on rap music, are you?"

"No, I hate it!" Al snapped. "Why?" Before the cherub could answer, the blaring, pulsating strains of rap tore through Al's ears. The singer, recording-studio tough, was yammering on about how his sneakers were cool and his guns were hot and the things he was going to do to the "hos" at his school.

The cherub pointed ahead, where Al could make out through the light a wide red strip, then one of purple, orange, yellow. . . . Soon he could make out an entire rainbow. The music seemed to be coming from the rainbow.

"Gee, thanks," Al murmured. "Just what I wanted to hear."

The cherub grinned impishly. "Look behind you."

Al turned. Floating directly behind him, at waist height, was a long wooden mallet. Al grabbed it—"Heavy but manageable," he thought. The cherub floated slowly toward the rainbow, beckoning Al to follow. When he reached the rainbow, Al recognized that it was the decorative art fronting an oversized, old-fashioned jukebox, which was vibrating and shaking to the heavy bass of the rap songs.

"Is this for what I think it is?" Al asked, indicating the mallet.

"My job is to get you in a better mood . . . a more positive frame of mind." The cherub smiled. "Here's a chance for you to get off to a happy start with us."

Al energetically raised the mallet and swung it forcefully into the crest of the jukebox. The glass shattered and the metal frame bent inward from the force of the blow. Sparks flew. The speakers were crushed. But the music continued to play, although the jukebox's programming was scorched; so the song began to play faster and faster, until it sounded like Alvin and the Chipmunks promising to cap some homeboy in the ass and bring down a wrath of lead onto any chump messing in their turf. Al gave the box a second bash and then a coup-de-grâce third whack. The machine collapsed in on itself and went silent.

"That was all right!" Al beamed, turning to the cherub, but he was gone.

Al could see another figure approaching him, so he dropped the mallet. Someone short . . . an older woman. She was wearing a shirt vaguely familiar to Al. It was a collared red shirt with the words *St. Mary's* written in white script across the front. People who worked at Al's grammar school wore that kind of shirt. "Please, God," Al thought, "don't let it be Mrs. Turtletaub again."

To Al's relief, he saw it was not. This woman was older, taller, and much more pleasing to look at.

"Hello, Master Mitchell," she called out as she approached him. "Do you remember me?" Al shook his head apologetically. "That's okay," she laughed. "I'm Mrs. Sludsucker!"

"Should I know you?" Al asked. The woman chuckled in response.

"I should hope so! Now that you have joined us up here, the first thing that happens is you meet the five most important people in your life. Starting with me!"

CHAPTER 7

adrian

"AL MITCHELL! WAKE up! Come on, Al! You'll have all eternity to rest!"

Al's eyelids opened. He shook away the grogginess and lifted his head cautiously. He was lying on a bed of beautifully polished wood. The wood floor was circular and seemed to be raised a few feet off the ground—just like a merry-go-round, only there were no horses to ride, no ornate designs to admire, just an empty flat disk of wood. The white light persisted around the perimeter of the disk, making it impossible for Al to see any farther than where the disk ended.

He dropped his head back down, banging the back of his skull on the hard wood, but again, strangely, it did not hurt. His head was fine and everything else felt good and seemed to be in working order . . . fingers, hands, toes, feet, arms, legs. He pulled himself to his feet and stretched, surveying his surroundings. He hadn't the foggiest idea how long he had spent with Mrs. Turtletaub, Pomeroy, Dr. Hammer, and his brother-in-law or the five strange people he met after destroying the jukebox.

"Nice of you to join the living . . . so to speak," said the voice that had awakened Al a few moments earlier. It was coming from the other side of the disk. Al had been myopic since the third grade, but now he could make out, with 20/20 precision, a diminutive man standing on the far end of the merry-go-round.

"Welcome," the little man said. "My name is Adrian." As he approached, Al could estimate with certainty that Adrian was only about five and a half feet tall; what was considerably less certain was Adrian's age. His face seemed very young, no wrinkles, pleasant features. He was more than clean-shaven; it looked as though he didn't grow facial hair at all. His eyes suggested an older, experienced man, a perception enhanced by the long silvery-white mane of hair on his head, which was pulled back and tied in a ponytail. He wore an immaculately tailored white suit trimmed in light blue. On one breast pocket was an ornately designed *H*.

"Hi. I'm Al Mitchell." Al extended his hand. Adrian smiled politely.

"No need for that, Mr. Mitchell," he said. "We know you have no weapons."

"What? Of course I'm not armed," Al said. "I just wanted to shake hands . . . you know, a friendly greeting."

"We don't shake hands up here." Adrian took Al by the arm and they began to slowly walk the perimeter of the disk. "Shaking hands is an earthbound custom devised centuries ago as a way for one man to assure another that he was not carrying a weapon in his hand. Since we have a policy up here of not allowing weapons of any kind, there is no need to shake hands."

"That's a policy? You have a policy up here?" Al was a bit surprised.

"That's right." Adrian smiled. "We have a policy . . . no weapons; no exceptions." Adrian flashed a mischievous wink at Al. "Plays havoc when members of the NRA get up here. But they get used to it. Did you rest well?"

"Yes, I think so," Al responded hesitantly. "I feel very good. How long was I sleeping?"

"How long?" Adrian looked at him curiously.

"Yes. How long was I asleep?" Al repeated.

"It doesn't matter. There is no time up here, Al. There's no need for it. The past, the present, the future . . . they all exist at this moment and in all moments simultaneously."

"That sounds like Einstein." Al laughed.

Adrian rolled his eyes.

"Don't remind me," Adrian said exasperatedly. "You can't believe how insufferable Einstein has been since he got up here and found out he was right. Time just doesn't matter up here. Of course, that news was a real downer for the president of the Swiss Watch Company when he got here. But, like the NRA guys, he got used to it."

Al gave Adrian the once-over. "Who are you?" Al asked.

"I told you. I am Adrian."

"I guess I should have asked you what you are."

"Why?"

"I don't know. You seem like a stand-up comedian." Al shrugged.

"What's the matter? Angels can't have a sense of humor?"

"So, you are an angel," Al said.

"No, I'm one of Madonna's backup dancers. Of course, I'm an angel. I hope you are going to be a little faster on the uptake, Al."

"Sorry. I'm still getting used to things."

"It's okay." Adrian gave him a reassuring slap on the back. "Now, I understand you just got through meeting with your five people. Was it helpful?"

"I'm not sure," Al said hesitantly.

"You are not sure about what?" Adrian asked.

"I'm not sure why I met the people I met."

"Wasn't it explained to you beforehand?" Adrian was betraying some annoyance. "You were supposed to meet the five people who most influenced your life, the five people who could best help you understand the meaning of your life."

"That was explained to me, yes." Al shrugged. "I just don't know why they picked the people they did."

"What was the matter with them?" Adrian asked.

"First, I met the sandwich lady from the cafeteria where I went to grammar school . . . St. Mary's. Believe me, Mrs. Sludsucker was a nice lady and all, but except for turning me on to roast beef when I was eight, she didn't have much of an impact on my life."

"That does seem pretty low on the importance meter, doesn't it?" Adrian said.

"The second person I met was our family plumber, Dave Moschkowitz. That was a surprise! I guess he was important because he taught me to use a plunger."

"That certainly has its uses." Adrian nodded.

"Also, on my eighteenth birthday, he turned me on to Miss Evelyn's House of Happiness on Route 35. Maybe I shouldn't talk about that up here."

"Probably a good idea not to," said Adrian.

"Then I met Misty Mangenello from Hoboken. She was my haircutter when I was in college. Nice girl. I asked her out a couple of times, but she always said no."

"How was she important in your life?" Adrian asked.

Al shrugged. "Only thing she ever helped me do was deal with my split ends."

"I'm afraid to ask about the other two people."

"The fourth person was a guy named Jorge Javier de la Valdivido. I didn't know him at all. He told me he was a flamenco dancer and part-time professional wrestler. He said I saw him dance at a Radio City Music Hall matinee, and that night I saw him wrestle as El Toreador at Madison Square Garden. He says I was the only person in history to see him dance and wrestle on the same day."

"That's one for the scrapbook, I guess." Adrian shrugged.

"The last person I met was Arnold Volk. He was a beekeeper who lived up the street from us when I was a kid. He was always warning everybody that the African killer bees were going to swarm over the United States by 1980 and turn us into drone laborers."

"I have to admit—a pretty colorful group," Adrian said admiringly. "But it doesn't sound like you met the right five people." Adrian pulled out a scroll from his belt and unfurled it. "Who is Ronald P. Dirkson?" he asked Al.

"My grandfather." Al smiled warmly. "He was a great guy. Now, *he* would have been one of the five people I should have met."

Adrian studied the scroll again. "How about Mollie Miniver?" he asked.

"My aunt Mollie . . . sure!" Al said. "She lived upstairs from us when I was a kid. She helped me through school more than my parents did."

Adrian grimaced, a little embarrassed.

"They were both supposed to meet you," he said. "Unfortunately, they were both meeting with other people whose lives they influenced and who got up here before you did. Sorry." Adrian checked over the scroll again. "I suppose you would have liked to see a fellow named Leif Nolton."

"Professor Nolton? Sure! He was my English professor in college; helped me become a writer and helped me land my first job."

"Yeah. Unfortunately, he couldn't meet with you either. He had to cancel last minute. He works in our Image Office."

"What's that?"

"The Image Office makes sure everything written about heaven is presented in a positive way. Unfortunately, Nolton seems to have gotten a last-minute request to look over a movie script about heaven that it looks like Spielberg wants to do."

Al scratched his head. Policies . . . PR department . . . stand-up comedians for angels . . . how much stranger could this get? "Heaven has a PR department?"

"Of course! It works pretty well, too. You ever hear anything bad said about heaven? Of course not! We're not going to let those revisionist historians and sociologists get ahold of heaven's reputation." Adrian pocketed the scroll. "I'm not going to bother with the last two names. They couldn't meet with you either. I'm afraid we owe you a big apology. You were the victim of overenthusiastic substitution."

"Victim of what?"

"I warned them this would happen! I told them there would be logistical problems with this program. But they wouldn't listen! They went ahead and did it anyway."

"Logistical problems?" Al asked, trying desperately to keep up with the conversation.

"Sure." Adrian tugged at Al's arm. "Come and walk with me, Al. I warned everybody that this five-people thing wasn't going to work. I told them. I said, 'Suppose one of the five people you want to meet is already meeting with someone else they influenced?' Just like your grandfather and aunt did today. Or suppose some of the five people aren't dead yet? Or, even worse, suppose some of them are . . ." Adrian paused and pointed downward, whispering, "down there."

"You mean hell?"

"No, I mean the ancient civilization thriving under my shoes," Adrian said sarcastically. "Of course, I mean hell."

"Don't get nasty. How am I supposed to know if hell exists or not?"

"Of course, it exists!" Adrian grinned. "There must be a hell if there is a heaven! You can't enjoy Friday unless there is a Monday, right? You can't enjoy Luciano Pavarotti unless there is an Ashlee Simpson. And you can't appreciate heaven unless there is a hell. That's the simplest rule of existence."

As they spoke, Adrian guided Al off the merry-go-round platform and through a sun-flooded glade of green grass and colorful wildflowers. They walked for what seemed to Al to be an interminable amount of time. But Al had no objections. He wasn't the least bit tired. No matter how far they walked, he felt no aches, no pains. In fact, every step through this incredibly beautiful scenery seemed to rejuvenate him.

"How long have we been walking?" Al asked Adrian.

"There you go with this time thing, again." Adrian shook his head. "You have to forget about time. It doesn't matter anymore."

"That takes some getting used to."

"Maybe you should consider joining this little support group we have called Clock Watchers Anonymous. It's very effective at teaching people to forget about time. I call it Tick-Tock Tech." Adrian pushed Al in the shoulder, grinning. "You get it?"

"Yes!" Al rolled his eyes.

"Or"—Adrian grinned—"we have a place where you can use time to work with wood. I call it Tick-Tock Teak." Adrian shot a glance at Al . . . still no reaction. "Or, of course, you could use time to steal things. That would be Tick-Tock Took. Or maybe play a children's game with time. Call it Tick-Tock Toe." Adrian waited again in vain for a reaction from Al, but none was forthcoming. "Oh! Come on, Al! This is funny stuff!"

"Are you going to do this for as long as we are walking?" Al said humorlessly.

"They told me you had a sense of humor!" Adrian pleaded. "What happened?"

"I still have it," Al said. "I save it for funny things."

"Well, then use it!" Adrian shouted. "If you can't laugh up here . . ." Adrian's voice trailed off, as he assumed Al caught his meaning.

Al looked at Adrian for a moment. He recalled Liz's comment to him at the Christmas party some years ago:

At least Dick Lynn tries to be funny!

"Al!" Adrian pleaded. "This is heaven! There is no reason not to feel good here all the time! This is as good as it gets!" Al mulled over Adrian's words a moment and finally broke into a broad grin. It was all right to feel happy again.

"Maybe my sense of humor got a little rusty," Al admitted. "Let's see if I can dust the cobwebs off it. You could use time to get an operation to reduce your stomach. Call it Tick-Tock Tuck."

"That's a good try!" Adrian pumped his fist in encouragement. "It's not funny, but it's a good try!"

"How about using time to teach proper manners?" Al asked. "That could be Tick-Tock Tact."

Adrian winced. "Maybe you were funnier when you didn't have a sense of humor."

Al continued on, ignoring Adrian. "Somebody from Constantinople who teaches time would be a Tick-Tock Turk."

The two men continued along, trading puns, their laughter echoing through the glade. After a short distance more, they came to the shoreline of a pristine, smooth-as-glass lake. In the distance, in the middle of the lake, they could see an island.

"That's where we're headed." Adrian pointed to the island.

"Okay," Al said cheerily, still walking until his feet were covered in the lapping water.

"What are you doing?" Adrian looked at him.

"I thought we were going to the island."

Adrian chuckled. "What did you think? You were going to walk out to the island?" Adrian looked incredulously at Al. "Who do you think you are? There's only one of us up here who can get across the lake that way! The rest of us have to take the bridge." Adrian pointed down the distant shoreline to where an elegantly arched bridge rose over the lake. Adrian took one more glance at Al and started laughing as he walked away.

"What's so funny?" Al asked defensively.

"You were going to try and walk across the lake!" Adrian laughed.

"I was not!" Al insisted. "How was I to know? I thought it was shallow water. I didn't even know it was a real lake!"

"Oh, come on!" Adrian continued to stay a few paces ahead of Al. "What are you talking about?"

"I thought it might be a fake lake!"

Adrian stopped and turned. "A fake lake? What would you make a fake lake out of?"

"I don't know! I'm new here. You didn't explain any of this to me!" Al said defensively.

Their bickering continued all the way down the shoreline and across the bridge. When they reached the other side, Adrian raised his hand for Al to keep his voice down.

"This is a serious place," he said in a strained whisper, then beckoned Al to follow him. They walked past hundreds of people, all in attire similar to Adrian's, their hair as white, their faces as smooth, featureless, and youthful, as his. They all sat on or behind glass desks, some looking very busy, others seemingly relaxed.

"This is where we administer the Five People You Meet in Heaven Program," Adrian continued to whisper. "I thought we would stop by and report the trouble you had. Some of heaven's best people work here." They walked a little farther into the island. Al noticed the center of the island was on an upward incline.

"You see that lady in the large red chair up at the top of the hill?" Adrian asked.

Al had already noticed her. She seemed to be in charge. She sat placidly in her chair, calmly watching all the activity on the island around her. The woman had the short and somewhat muscular proportions of a weight lifter. She did not have white hair. Hers was dark, wild, and tangled, falling along her shoulders.

"You know who that is?" Adrian asked, with his best I-have-a-secret face.

"Cleopatra?" Al guessed. Adrian shook his head. "Joan of Arc?"

"Older than that," Al replied. "That's Eve."

Al turned to Adrian. "You mean *the* Eve? As in the mother-of-the-human-race Eve?"

"Sure do."

"Wow! That's Eve?" Al said again, as if trying to convince himself of the reality of it.

"What do you think?" Adrian asked.

"She's not really a looker," Al said quietly, looking around nervously as if expecting to be punished for saying that about such a prominent biblical personality.

"No, I guess not"—Adrian nodded—"but very sturdy . . . very strong . . . very practical. All the things you need in the first woman of a race, I guess."

"I'd like to meet her," Al said excitedly. "Can you introduce me? Does she know you?"

"She doesn't know me from Adam." Adrian paused, then blurted out a self-congratulatory laugh. "God, I love to do that to people."

CHAPTER 8

kinks

A S THEY WALKED out of Eve's range of view, Adrian pointed
to a man sitting motionlessly under a tree.

"See that fellow? Do you know who he is?" The man wore a
long brown monk's robe, but other than that, he gave no indication
of his identity.

"Looks like he's a monk," Al replied.

"Guys like him are the reason meeting five people in heaven
isn't working as well as it should," Adrian explained. "He's a monk.
His name is Mastriannio. He lived in Italy in the fifteenth century.
His parents abandoned him at an alpine monastery when he was an
infant, so the monks took him in. Mastriannio decided to live a life

of voluntary seclusion so he could constantly worship God. He never met five people in his entire life. What can we do with him? And he's not the only one. Look over there."

Adrian pointed to a young man in a Japanese World War II military uniform meticulously shaping some shrubbery.

"That's Karatsu Hashimitsu. His father was a captain in the Japanese army during World War II—one of those gung ho types who hid on an island for fifty years after the war ended because he never got the word. You would think his father would have figured it out when he stopped getting orders from his superiors or when the Japanese navy stopped showing up or when American corporations began opening offices all over the island. Karatsu was born illegitimately in 1944 and lived in hiding with his father and mother for twenty years. Then he got beriberi, which sent him to that great hibachi grill in the sky."

The amount of workers and desks began to thin out as Al and Adrian reached the far end of the island. They passed one particular desk where a group of people were engaged in an animated discussion.

"What are they getting so heated about?" Al asked.

"That's the Reincarnation Desk. We had a guy come up this morning who insists he lived five other lives . . . six all together. We have to decide whether he gets visited by five people or thirty people. We figure we better get this straightened out before Shirley MacLaine gets up here."

Adrian pointed to the last desk near the island shoreline. The tall, lean man who occupied the desk was hunched over, deep in thought. A small triangular wood-carved nameplate identified this as the Five People You Meet in Heaven Complaint Desk. Adrian approached the desk and banged on it.

"Wake up, Magnolia!" Adrian shouted. The man behind the desk lifted his head slowly, not startled at all by Adrian's ruckus.

"Hello, Adrian," Magnolia said in a deep but syrupy sweet southern drawl. "For your information, I was not sleeping, just thinking." Like Adrian, Magnolia had no telltale signs of aging; he seemed youthful and vigorous, and yet, at the same time, in no particular hurry. Unlike Adrian, he was very tall and his white hair was shaved like a crew cut, closely cropped around his head. Magnolia listened patiently as Adrian reviewed the problems Al had with the five people he was supposed to meet.

"Looks like we haven't worked out all the kinks," Magnolia acknowledged, turning to Al. "If you like, we can reconstitute the program for you and reschedule the five people to meet with you now."

"You don't have to go through all that trouble for me."

"Good." Magnolia nodded approvingly. "I never put much mind to this program anyway. I mean . . . I don't need five people . . . no matter who they are . . . to tell me about my life and what it meant. I think I'm smart enough to figure that out on my own. I reckon you are smart enough, too, Al."

"I guess so—" Al replied, but Magnolia kept talking.

"I don't trust all this new touchy-feely stuff we're doing up here. This whole Five People You Meet in Heaven is pretty new. Did you know that, Al?"

"No—"

"Only started doing it a couple of hundred years ago. Don't know why. Everybody who came up here before the program did just fine. Julius Caesar didn't have to meet five people to know what he was all about, did he, Adrian? Or Alexander the Great.

Even Attila the Hun!" Magnolia put his hand up to his mouth to hide an embarrassed grin. "Truth is, nobody would have met with old Attila anyway. Smelled like a Dumpster behind a Mexican restaurant. Never bathed. And that breath!" Magnolia rolled his eyes. "The Almighty invented toothpaste and sent it down to earth because of that crazy Hun. Did you know that, Al?"

"No, again." Al looked to Adrian for help.

"True story." Adrian shrugged.

"You are a good man, Al," Magnolia said, standing up and shaking his hand. "I'll leave you with Adrian here. He'll take care of you from this point onward."

CHAPTER 9

le morte de merry-go-round

A L AND ADRIAN were walking back across the bridge.

"What did Magnolia mean when he said you were going to take care of me?" Al wondered aloud.

"How about we take a walk at Seafarer Beach?" Adrian suggested.

Before Al could answer, he was standing on the boardwalk, out in front of the Roundabout. Police cars and an ambulance were stationed by the entrance, their whirling emergency lights cutting through the darkening night. A crowd of onlookers were trying to get a glimpse of the activities inside. Adrian and Al walked right through the crowd to the entranceway without consequence or detection. Just as Al began peering inside, a police officer emerged from the doorway, plowing the crowd aside. Dick Lynn, Sandy Trent, and Paul Gergen, each with arms around the other for comfort, followed behind him. When they had made their way through the crowd, they paused to recover.

"I can't believe it!" Sandy groaned. "He just went for a walk."

"How can he get killed on a merry-go-round?" Paul asked acerbically. "On a merry-go-round! He's been on the Lightning Loops and the Thrill Drill and the CentraForce a hundred times . . . and he gets killed on the merry-go-round?"

"Hard to believe, isn't it?" Sandy dabbed at the tear in her eye.

"There's no explaining it." Dick Lynn shook his head.

"It was a freak accident!" Al shouted self consciously, but only Adrian could hear him. When Adrian didn't react, Al repeated himself. "It was a freak accident!"

"If you say so," said Adrian.

Meanwhile, the policeman who had escorted Al's friends through the crowd came up to Dick.

"We will bring the body down to the morgue. You can tell whoever is going to claim the body to claim it there."

"I don't think he has any family in the area. His parents are in Florida. I'll let them know." The policeman nodded, but instead of walking away, it seemed there was something else he wanted to say. "Something else?" Dick asked.

"Sorry for your loss," the policeman said, fighting off a slight grin. "But in twenty years on the force, I've never heard of a case where someone was killed by a merry-go-round." The policeman looked befuddled. "How can you be killed by a merry-go-round?"

Al's shoulders sagged. "Another smart-ass," he said dryly to Adrian.

Dick decided not to respond, so the policeman began urging the crowd to disburse. Slowly, reluctantly, the crowd that had gathered at the entrance to the Roundabout thinned. An old woman who stood closest to the entranceway turned to the people nearest her.

"Since 1932, this ride had been running," the old woman said, her face in a wistful reflection. "Thousands and thousands of kids have been on it without nobody ever getting hurt . . . until tonight." Everybody shook their heads solemnly. Without missing a beat, the old woman continued in a suddenly effusive voice. "What kind of moron gets himself killed on a damn merry-go-round?" With that, the old woman and the crowd around her burst into laughter as they obliviously filed past Al and Adrian.

"Very funny!" Al shouted after the crowd. "Hope you all have a good time!" Al turned and gave Adrian his best "Et tu, Brute?" look—Adrian, who was having a hard time suppressing his own laughter.

"Oh, you think it's funny, too?" Al asked.

"Well, let's face it, Al; it's not every day someone is killed by a merry-go-round." Adrian began to giggle. "Killed by a merry-go-round," he repeated, laughing harder. "Death by merry-go-round!" Adrian burst out in a gut-busting laugh. He noticed Al wasn't amused. "Come on! Remember what we said before! You have to lighten up . . . get that sense of humor back!" He started laughing again. "I'm sorry. I can't help it!" Adrian struggled to talk through the laughs.

"Come on, Al! Lighten up! It's funny! Really! If you think about it! We could put out an all-points bulletin. . . . You know . . . if you see this merry-go-round, take no action yourself, but call local law enforcement." Adrian doubled over. "We could put up a WANTED poster in the post office . . . or do a story on *America's Most Wanted*!" Adrian deepened his voice to imitate a television announcer. "Tonight, on *America's Most Wanted,* a killer merry-go-round and a flying horse combine to spin a ride of death in New Jersey!" Adrian resumed his normal voice, still gasping for breath between laughs. "Wait! You could write your memoirs, Al. Call them *Le Morte de Merry-Go-Round.*" Adrian screamed out laughing again.

Al turned to him, his face dour.

"I hope you're having a good time!" Adrian caught his breath, almost immediately feeling sorry for Al, and started out after him.

"Sorry, Al." Adrian caught up to him on the boardwalk, successfully suppressing his last giggle. "But you have to admit—"

"Look," Al snapped, "I'm sure I'm not the first person to ever die on a merry-go-round. . . ."

"No." Adrian nodded. "You're not. Close to it, though. There are only two other recorded deaths on merry-go-rounds in human history. The first is a really sad story. This old guy in Kansas City keeled over from a heart attack while riding with his wife. They were celebrating a special anniversary. Seems they consummated their marriage on this very same merry-go-round fifty years earlier, and this old guy was planning one more ride—and I don't mean on the horse.

"The other case was this guy who helped build one of the first merry-go-rounds ever—on the pier at Atlantic City. During a test ride, this guy got his head caught in one set of gears and his leg caught in another and the gears slowly pulled him apart. It didn't turn out well for him, but it gave one of the witnesses the idea to invent saltwater taffy."

"Thanks, Adrian," Al said. "I can't tell you how much better I feel now."

harp

A L TOOK A seat on a bench opposite the Roundabout enclosure. It gave him a clear, expansive view of the ocean. Adrian stood behind him.

"I can't believe you brought me all the way back here to laugh at the klutzy way I killed myself!"

"I didn't," Adrian replied. "I brought you here to tell you some good news. I think it will cheer you up, Al." Adrian circled around the bench and sat down next to Al, slapping him on the knee enthusiastically. "You qualify for a very special program!"

"I do?" Al asked. "What kind of program? Don't tell me heaven has one of those Publishers Clearing House things."

"No," Adrian reassured him, with another pat on the knee. "Look, during your years on earth, the average human male's life expectancy was about eighty-four years. You only achieved a little more than half that. Also, your life by almost any measure was not a very happy one."

"That's an understatement."

"Add to that the problem with the Five People You Meet in Heaven Program, and, guess what? You are eligible to participate in HARP."

"I don't want to play the harp." Al dismissed Adrian with a wave and stood up.

Adrian grabbed him by the belt and forced him back onto the bench. "It's not about playing the harp," he said, laughing. "The last thing we need up here is you playing the harp. No. HARP is a new heavenly program we developed to help you."

"How the hell will it help me?" asked an impatient Al.

"Al," Adrian whispered a cautionary note. "Watch your language. You may think we're on the boardwalk . . . but remember where we really are." Adrian resumed his full voice. "HARP is a program we offer to people like you who basically were good people but had a short, unhappy life; sort of a way of making things up to you."

"What is HARP?"

"The Heavenly Angels' Restitution Program. It gives you the chance to exact restitution from five people who made your life on earth so difficult."

Al was suddenly intrigued.

"What do you mean, 'exact restitution'? You mean . . . revenge? Vengeance?"

"We prefer to think of it as restitution, Al. Sounds a bit more appropriate for heaven, don't you think?" Adrian shook his head bemusedly. "At first, we called it the Corporeal Revenge Administration Program, but nobody liked the word *revenge* in there . . . too harsh. And the head angels thought there was a major problem with the acronym."

"You are telling me that I can get even with the five biggest jerks I knew on earth?" Al said, still not quite believing what he was hearing. "I didn't think you guys encouraged this kind of thing. I thought you guys were more about, you know, love thy neighbor, turn the other cheek, and all that stuff."

Adrian raised his eyebrow.

"'Vengeance is mine. . . . I will repay,' sayeth the Lord," Adrian said softly. "You've heard that, haven't you? Ask the people in Sodom and Gomorrah if God is into revenge. How about Noah's flood or Lot's wife turning into a pillar of salt? Don't forget the Egyptian army and the Red Sea."

"Okay . . . okay . . . I get the picture."

"And don't worry," Adrian said. "HARP is still a pretty small program, so you won't have to worry about a lot of screwups."

"Geez, acronyms . . . programs . . . policies . . . PR departments . . . screwups. . . . It sounds like heaven is one huge bureaucracy," Al said.

"You don't know the half of it, Al," Adrian winked. "We've got a big bureaucracy because we have so much to handle. We have departments that handle solicited requests by prayer, unsolicited requests by prayer, solicited requests made without prayer, solicited requests by clergy, by nonclergy, believers, nonbelievers, sometime believers, believers-only-because-they-want-their-requests-fulfilled, late-to-the-party-believers-because-they-are-about-to-die-and-think-they-are-screwed. We have departments that handle group requests, individual requests, family requests, nationwide requests, tribal requests, parish requests. You can't believe how many requests we get every day. And that's just from planet Earth! I used to think God didn't grant everybody's prayers because he wanted man to suffer some hardships as a way to build character. But the real reason is that most of the requests to him get lost in the paper shuffle."

"Wow! I had no idea!"

"We aren't going to let HARP get bogged down in bureaucracy like that. All you have to do is pick the five jerks and we will get going."

"Good deal!" Al jumped up. "I'm ready!"

"Hold on one moment." Adrian grabbed him by his belt again and brought him back down onto the bench once more. "HARP has some very strict rules you must adhere to."

"Rules? What rules?"

"The kind of rules you would expect. No murder, attempted murder, assault, battery, pillaging, raping, stoning, or other act that can cause physical, psychological, or physiological harm; no outright threats or material alterations to the life or lifestyle of the subject or the subject's family thereof; no committing of a crime or entrapment on your part to entice a subject to commit a crime in the fulfilling of the restitution. You may not call upon, or seem to call upon, or intimate help from Satan, any devil, or devil's minion, recognized or otherwise."

"Wow! Doesn't sound like there's much I can do."

"There are lots of things to do." Adrian turned to Al and gave him an impishly evil smile. "Trust me. That's what I am here to help you with, Al . . . to help you get your restitution. It's my specialty."

CHAPTER 11

the first jerk al mitchell meets on earth

THE SWIRLING WHITE mist returned and it enveloped Al and Adrian until they could no longer see the boardwalk or the ocean. When it cleared, Al found himself sitting next to Adrian in the first row of a dimly lit musty old theater. Al tried to shift his weight, but it was difficult. The fabric on his seat was ripped and the springs were shot, causing him to sink uncomfortably low in the chair. Adrian was not doing much better. His seat back was cracked and reclining and he had all he could do to sit upright.

A row of emergency bulbs embedded in the floor along the center aisle provided the only light in the theater. The darkness made it impossible to see anything except the stage in front of them. The remnants on the stage evoked the early age of television, a flimsy podium, a few leather chairs, some old-fashioned black-and-white cameras, and a set of standing floodlights.

"The theater's not much to look at"—Adrian pulled himself out of the chair and sat on the armrest—"but it has a heck of a lot of character." As he spoke, Adrian produced a wallet-sized silver device from his pocket that glowed a luminescent green as he held it up to his face. With a flick of his wrist, the top half of the device flipped open. "Kirk to *Enterprise,*" Adrian said dramatically, then began laughing. "I love doing that!"

"What is that thing?" Al asked.

"This?" Adrian held up the device. "This is the Alexandria Library of the information age." Al gave him a puzzled look. "You've heard of the Library of Alexandria? It was reputed to have amassed all the knowledge humans had collected to that point in time." Adrian held up the gadget. "That's what this is. A repository for all we know about everything. We call it the HEAVEN box— for Heaven Entertainment and Virtually Everything Network."

"Does everybody have one of those?"

"Eventually everyone up here gets one, yes." Adrian lowered his voice. "You have to keep it quiet, though. We don't want Microsoft coming up here and slapping a logo on it."

"Why are we in this old theater?" Al asked.

"This is where they filmed a lot of old TV game shows like *The Price Is Right.* You know . . ." Adrian began shouting, "'Come on Down!' I always loved that show. Of course, I liked *Charlie's Angels* more, but none of them are up here yet. Anyway, I thought it would be more fun to do our work here than sitting at my desk."

"What do we do?" Al asked.

"Tell me the first person you want us to HARP on."

"I'm going back to my childhood." Al involuntarily clenched his teeth. "A jerk of a kid named Butch Lowe."

"Okay!" Adrian repeated the name directly into his HEAVEN box and waited a moment. "Well, you're in luck. Butch Lowe is still on earth." Adrian curled another devilish grin on his lips. "Now watch this!"

Suddenly a row of lights in each corner of the ceiling flashed on and began throwing bright spotlights all around the theater like it was a major Hollywood premiere. The floodlights on the stage burst into full luminescence, blinding Al for a moment. An unseen orchestra blasted a regal fanfare and an announcer's voice blared over the loudspeaker system with over-the-top enthusiasm, "Butch Lowe! *Come on Down!*" A crescendo of applause followed as a holographic 3-D image of a young boy, nine, maybe ten, years old floated down the aisle, stopping in front of the stage. The kid was burly and big-eared, with unkempt hair and a sly, almost cocky, smile, and he began to rotate slowly in front of the stage. The announcer's voice tore through the loudspeakers again. "Let's say hello to our first subject, Hiram Lowe, known to his friends as Butch. Born in 1962, Butch wasn't Mister Congeniality. In fact, he parlayed an aggressive personality into a fairly successful high school football career. He was also a wrestler and a swimmer, two sports in which he did a lot better than in football."

"Hiram?" Al turned to Adrian. "His name is Hiram? We always thought his first name was Butch!"

"Maybe that's why he was such a jerk." Adrian put the HEAVEN box back into his pocket. "How would you like to be called Hi Lowe all your life?"

The announcer continued. "Butch is now forty-four years old and lives in New Hope, Pennsylvania. He tends bar evenings at a pub called the Gnarled Limb. He's divorced; his wife and son live in upstate New York." Butch's image slowly began to morph into a hefty middle-aged man, grizzled, mostly bald, his smile revealing a few missing teeth both top and bottom, his eyes revealing a darker, meaner sort than his nine-year-old counterpart.

"Is that how Butch Lowe looks today?" Al asked.

"No, that's the cover model for this year's *Sports Illustrated* swimsuit issue," Adrian responded dryly. "Yes, that's what Butch looks like today. Tell me why he's such a jerk."

"Okay," Al responded softly, almost secretively. "When I was twelve, I had the best paper route in the county—two apartment buildings at the end of our street—three hundred apartments, almost all senior citizens and almost all subscribers. It was so easy . . . no bicycling around in the rain or snow . . . just up and down the elevator in the apartments. Then I go and open my big mouth at school and I tell some friends of mine what easy money I'm making. They blab it around and the very next day, the trouble started. . . ."

November 1974

Twelve-year-old Al Mitchell, an impatient bundle of energy, tapped his foot as he watched the needle slowly measure the downward progress of the elevator from fifth floor to fourth, fourth to third, and so on. The elevator was painfully slow, and the apartment building old, but if anyone complained, old Mr. Schneider, the superintendent, would just smile and say they were lucky the building wasn't twenty or thirty stories tall.

Finally, the elevator passed the second floor and settled at the lobby. The doors began to open slowly. Al slipped through them and practically danced across the marble floor of the lobby, the generous weight of the tips loading down his right pocket. He pushed through the front door of the building and out into the chilling late-day November air. A few more lucrative days like this and he would be able to afford anything he wanted.

The pair of brick apartments stood alone at the end of Al's street next to an undeveloped lot of oak and maple trees. Al had to pass by this lot to get home, and as he pedaled toward it, he was surprised to see Butch Lowe sitting on a low-hanging oak-tree branch just a few feet in front of him. Al didn't want to say anything to Butch—in fact, he was hoping to get by him without even having to acknowledge his presence. They weren't exactly bosom buddies.

"Hey! Mitchell!" Butch bellowed. "Don't you want to know why I'm in this tree?"

"Because somebody planted an acorn in your ass twelve years ago?" Al picked up the pace, trying to pedal past Lowe, but the wrestler was too fast. He jumped from the tree and landed right next to Al, grabbing hold of the handlebars.

"Hold on, buddy! I was waiting to see you! Get off the bike a minute, will you?"

"Why?" Al asked suspiciously. Al tried to back away on the bike, but he couldn't move fast enough

to break Butch's grip. Butch wrestled the handlebars
to the side, forcing the bicycle to fall over. Al couldn't
keep his balance and he went down to the ground
with it. Al figured he'd better get up quickly, but Lowe,
again lightning quick, closed the gap between the two
of them and grabbed Al's arm, twisting it around
behind him. Using this leverage, Butch prevented Al
from getting up. Al grunted more in frustration than
in pain.

"You know what I heard on the radio this morning,
Mitchell? There was this commercial for insurance.
You know what insurance is, Mitchell?"

"I guess you are going to tell me."

"It's money you pay to make sure bad things don't
happen to you," Butch said. "That's what I wanted to talk
to you about. I think you need to get some insurance."

"Why?" Al grunted.

"Because, if you don't pay for insurance, something
bad could happen to you . . . like a broken arm." Butch
bent Al's arm up and farther out of position.

"Cut it out, Butch!" Al was pleading more than
demanding.

"Would you pay for insurance against a broken
arm, Mitchell."

"Why should I?" Al grunted.

"You know, it only takes seven pounds of pressure to
break an arm. That's not much." Butch pushed Al's arm
a bit farther out of position. Al could feel his arm was
about to snap.

"Okay! Okay! I'll pay!" Al shouted. Butch released Al's arm.

"You know, all the guys at school say you're a dumb cluck"—Lowe chuckled, helping a reluctant Al to his feet—"but I knew you were smart."

"What do you want?" Al asked.

"Word is you got hundreds of customers in the apartments. Is that right?" Al stared stone-faced. Butch didn't care. "You average . . . what? Fifty cents from each as a tip? That's fifty dollars! I want thirty. Right now! You give me thirty dollars, and you don't get your arm broke." Butch stood smugly, his hands on his hips, as Al reluctantly dug into his weighty pocket. He peeled off thirty single dollars and pushed it quickly into Butch's hand, pocketing the rest before Butch could grab that, too.

"All right!" Butch howled gleefully and pulled Al into a headlock. "You collect every other Thursday, right? That means that every other Thursday, you pay me thirty dollars and then I don't break your arm! See how easy?" Al didn't respond, so Butch squeezed harder on his head.

"Yes! Okay!" Al shouted. Butch released him and dug into his own pocket, pulling out a cherry Tootsie Roll pop. He unwrapped it and slipped it into his mouth. To complete the humiliation, Butch pinched Al's cheek. "Who loves ya, baby!" Butch chuckled and ran away.

"Who loves ya, baby!" Al repeated snidely, slumping in his theater seat. "Butch said that to me every time I gave him the money. *Kojak* was his favorite TV show. I haven't been able to look at Telly Savalas my whole life without getting sick."

"Why didn't you get somebody to help you?"

"Like who?" Al responded, suddenly reliving the desperation he felt at the time. "If I told my parents, they'd tell Butch's parents, they'd punish Butch, and then he'd beat the hell out of me. If I told a teacher, the teacher would keep Butch after school and then Butch would beat the hell out of me. If I told the police, what do you think Butch would have done?"

"Probably killed you," Adrian said.

"Exactly. You notice there's a pattern here?"

"How long did this go on?" Adrian asked as he pulled out his HEAVEN box again.

"I don't know. A few months. Then, I quit the route and he left me alone."

"It went on for thirty-six weeks." Adrian studied the screen of his HEAVEN box and shook his head disapprovingly. "You made eighteen payments. That's five hundred and forty dollars."

"I can't describe the feeling I had, giving Butch the money."

"Would that feeling be humiliation?" Adrian offered.

"Yeah, that's it. Thanks for the help."

"Didn't you ever want to fight him?"

"At the time, no. He would have beaten the hell out of me. After I quit the paper route, I took a karate course. Within a month I could chop a cinder block in half with my bare hands."

"Great!" Adrian said. "That explains why you never got robbed by any renegade cinder blocks." Adrian suddenly clapped his hands. "Hey! I think we found something!"

"What?" Al said, trying to get a look at the HEAVEN screen.

Adrian pulled it out of Al's view. "Sorry. You can't use one of these yet. But it looks like Butch Lowe once was a swimmer in college!"

"He was a very competitive athlete in everything . . . football, wrestling—"

"But most especially swimming!" Adrian closed the HEAVEN box. "It looks like he was a champion swimmer at one time. And, it seems, Butch is working the late shift tonight at the Gnarled Limb."

"What does that mean?"

"It means we've found a way to HARP on Mr. Hi Lowe."

New Hope, Pennsylvania, sits in the foothills of the Pocono Mountains along the Delaware River, about forty miles north of Philadelphia and about ten miles north of where George Washington and his troops made their famous Christmas night crossing of the Delaware River in 1776. The streets of New Hope are angular and curved, not friendly to modern vehicular traffic, and each street is higher than the last as you move inward from the river.

New Hope is a study in comedic extremes. Its Main Street has some of the most populated biker bars in the Mid-Atlantic states. It is common in New Hope to hear the ear-splitting revving of motorcycle engines echoing off the hillside. It is equally common to see dozens of motorcycles parked along the street and their black-leather-clad owners greeting each other and sharing some beers.

Strangely, a world of the opposite extreme coexists peacefully with this bikers' haven, for New Hope is the Greenwich Village of Pennsylvania. Main Street and many of the nooks and crannies of its side streets are peppered with boutiques, specialty shops, art galleries, taverns, and nouvelle-riche restaurants that draw the sport-coat-and-turtleneck "arts and entertainment" crowd.

Many of these establishments occupy buildings that predate the Revolutionary War. A good example is the Gnarled Limb. The original building, built in 1745, was a boathouse and tavern. It was set well back off Main Street, where it abutted the Delaware River. Colonials would use the services of a boat or barge to cross the Delaware from this spot, and if they had to wait for their ride, they could kill some time with a hot applejack or rum at the bar.

Today, the Gnarled Limb is a tavern, as well as a restaurant, and it maintains the look and character of its origins, showcasing small handblown glass windows, thick timber beams running the length of the ceiling, hardwood floors, and various working fireplaces to warm the rooms.

Adrian held the thick oak door open for Al as they entered the Gnarled Limb. Being over six feet tall, Al had to crouch down to protect his head from hitting the timbers. It was very late—almost two-thirty in the morning—and the L-shaped bar that dominated the room was empty except for two woozy regulars camped on bar stools near the door. Al and Adrian took two barstools at the opposite end. At the moment, there was no one behind the bar.

"You sure this is right?" Al whispered to Adrian.

"Patience." Adrian winked and looked across at the two regulars studying them. "Good evening," Adrian shouted. The two men curled their lips into insincere smiles in response. Moments later, a human hurricane came barreling through the swinging door behind the bar. He was holding a tray full of dirty plates and glasses, which he carelessly dumped into a sink full of dishwater.

Sure enough, it was none other than Butch Lowe. Lowe started washing the glasses, oblivious to his new customers until one of the regulars said something that caused Butch to turn around. He did not look happy—grabbing a towel to dry his hands, then slamming it down in disgust.

"Closing time's in thirty minutes," Lowe growled through a half-smoked, half-chewed cigar. "I'm just warning you because when we close, we close prompt-like." Butch approached the two, his eyes beginning to study Al's face curiously. "Usually we only get regulars in here this late and they know the routine."

"Don't worry, barkeep," Adrian said cheerfully. "We won't spoil your routine." Adrian banged his hands on the bar. "Seven and seven for me."

"Vodka tonic," Al murmured without looking directly at Butch. Any minute, he was sure, Butch would pull him over the bar and put him back into a headlock. Lowe began mixing the drinks without taking his eyes off Al.

"You look familiar somehow," Butch said. "You been in here before?"

"First time," Al said weakly.

"Sure is something familiar-looking about you." Butch slammed the drinks on the bar and went back to washing the glasses. Adrian and Al watched Butch converse with the two regulars and carry on as he probably did every normal night of his bartending life. Al sensed Adrian was biding his time, waiting for the right moment to do whatever it was he came here to do. Finally, after about fifteen minutes, Adrian pointed to the newspaper clippings framed on the wall behind the bar. With his newly minted 20/20 eyesight, Al could see they were all about Butch's college swimming championships.

"Hey, barkeep! How about two more here?" Adrian called.

Butch wandered over reluctantly.

"Last call," he said, grabbing both their glasses.

"Hey, barkeep! That you?" Adrian pointed to the newspaper clippings.

"Yeah," Butch replied, his tone unmistakably conveying his lack of interest in conversing. He put the new drinks on the bar. "That's me."

"I was a champion swimmer, too!" Adrian beamed.

"When?" Butch guffawed. "During the Civil War?" The two wobbling patrons at the end of the bar joined in Butch's laughter.

"That's very funny," Adrian conceded good-naturedly. "No, I was a swimmer about thirty years ago . . . at Princeton University." As soon as Butch heard that, the smile disappeared and the laughter stopped. Not concerned, Adrian held up his glass. "Cheers!" He finished the drink in one gulp.

"Princeton swimmer, huh?" Butch asked.

"Yes!" Adrian replied. "Who did you swim for? I cannot read it on the clipping."

"Eastern Pennsylvania Technical College." Butch folded his arms in a "you-want-to-make-something-of-it" pose.

"Eastern PA College? I remember them!" Adrian turned to Al. "We used to beat the crap out of them every year!" Butch sauntered over to Adrian. Al tensed, expecting that Butch would come over the bar at him any moment.

"So you swam for Princeton . . . what'd you do? Practice in a heated pool in your daddy's backyard?"

"Actually, we didn't need a heated pool," Adrian smiled. "We built ours indoors . . . in a room off the conservatory. Thank goodness we had such a big house." Butch stared coldly, then turned his back on Adrian, who gave Al a playful wink. "Hey!" he called to Butch. "I was a national champion . . . three years running in the medley relay, the breaststroke, and the freestyle." Butch turned and nodded.

"Congratulations," he said without the slightest pretense of sincerity.

"I see you were champion two years." Adrian giggled derisively. "Nice try."

"Adrian," Al whispered. "What are you trying to do?"

"Yeah?" Butch turned and closed the space between him and Adrian as quickly as he had with Al in front of the apartment buildings so many years ago. "Maybe if my daddy was a member of the country club, and I had Daddy's money to get me a big indoor pool, and probably a coach to teach me and wipe my ass, I might have won a third year, too."

"Maybe. But you didn't." Adrian examined the glass in his hand, seemingly unaware or unconcerned about the increasing agitation of the burly bartender. "Besides, just to set the record straight, the coach wiped my ass for free." Butch's face was turning redder and redder.

"Easy there, Butch," one of the regulars called. "You know what the police said would happen if they have to come here again." Heeding the words, Butch backed away and took a deep breath.

"You know what I think?" Adrian turned to Al, obviously not relenting. "I think our barkeep is a little angry about the fact I went to a rich school and he went to a . . . how shall we phrase it . . . a monetarily challenged institution."

"Keep talking," Butch challenged.

"We knew they were a poor school because everybody on their swim team shared the same bathing suit." Adrian laughed, while

Al grimaced. "I don't think Eastern PA had its own pool. I think they practiced in the fountain by the front entrance."

"Hey, Princeton!" Butch cut in. "You want to know where I did my practicing?"

"I was going to guess your bathtub, but just looking at you, there's no way you saw the inside of a bathtub that frequently. I give up. Where did you practice?"

"Right out back, Mr. Smart-ass. In the Delaware, down by Washington's Crossing."

"I hope you said hi to George and the boys as you swam by," Adrian cracked. One of the tipsy regulars cackled a laugh, which stopped the instant Butch whirled and looked at him.

"From one side to the other and back again," Butch continued, turning again to Adrian, "ten months a year, every day rain or shine, warm or cold . . . with the current or against the current. I could swim the river in eight minutes."

"I could do it in seven." Adrian shrugged casually.

"Bull!" Butch slammed the bar so hard, the rest of Al's drink splashed up and onto it.

"It's amazing what Princeton training can do, isn't it?"

Butch was flushed. He pulled the cigar from his mouth and jabbed it at Adrian's face.

"How much is that Princeton training worth to you now? How about you and me go down to Washington's Crossing Park right now and test it out?"

"You want to race me across the Delaware River tonight?" Adrian asked.

"What do you say, Mr. Princeton hotshot?" Butch pulled out his wallet and held up a series of one-hundred-dollar bills. "First one across wins a thousand dollars!" The two regulars near the bar shouted and whistled their approval.

"I won't swim against you for money." Adrian shook his head.

"I didn't think so." Butch smirked. "Coward."

Adrian smiled calmly. "I didn't say I wouldn't swim against you. I just won't do it for money."

"Because you know you'll lose!" One of the patrons shouted across the bar, getting a satisfied nod from Butch.

"Hardly, sir," Adrian said calmly. "I am willing to do it to uphold the honor of my name and my college." He peered directly into Butch's eyes. "You obviously have a deep-seated dislike for my school, and I assume a deep-seated loyalty to your own. If that's the case, then prove you are better for the sake of ol' Eastern PA and your reputation. That's more important than winning some money." Butch put the cigar—or what was left of it—back into his mouth and gnawed on it for a few seconds.

"You're on!" he shouted. His two regular patrons howled and applauded.

"There is only one problem," Adrian said. "Obviously I didn't know this was going to happen. I don't have a suit."

Butch's face contorted with howls of laughter. "Neither do I, Princeton boy! Who needs one? It'll be four in the morning! In March. Believe me, no one's in the park at that hour." Butch turned to his friends. "Finish up, boys, we're closing."

Al finished his drink and leaned over to Adrian. "This is it? This is how I get my revenge? By having you outswim him?"

"Patience, Al." Adrian stood and whipped some money onto the bar. "It will all be clear to you soon."

"How do you know you can beat him?"

Adrian just smiled and headed for the door.

℮ ⌐ Washington's Crossing Park sits on both sides of the Delaware River, a nationally hallowed spot replete with colonial period buildings and stores preserved as they originally were. Both sides of the park have ample tree-lined lawns and walking paths. Stone markers approximate where Washington's army embarked from the Pennsylvania side and where it landed on the New Jersey side in the sleet and snow of a historic winter. At the point of the crossing, the river is about sixty feet wide, with a mean, unrelenting southward current. A steel bridge wide enough for a single lane of traffic traverses the river a few hundred feet south of the markers.

Al was slowly driving over that bridge to the New Jersey side, careful not to attract the attention of the one park ranger Adrian said would be on duty at that time. As he came to the end of the bridge, he glanced at the backseat, where both men had thrown their clothes. Each had donned a white cotton towel that Butch had brought from the bar. Al shot a glance into the small guard shack standing at the end of the New Jersey side of the bridge. It was empty. Al checked his watch. It was almost four in the morning. The park ranger was either asleep or on patrol. Al assumed the former.

Passing the guard station, Al turned the car sharply left and negotiated a hairpin turn that brought him down a steeply sloped roadway and into a gravel parking lot adjacent to the river. He pulled the car as close to the river's edge as he dared, turned on the high beams and the car heater, and got out, leaving his door open. He rushed over to the other side of the car and opened the front passenger-side door, as Adrian had instructed. The headlights shimmered across the darkness of the river like horizontal spotlights.

After a few moments, the two towel-clad men walked into the light and took their positions standing on the opposite side of the river along the last few feet of Pennsylvania.

Al wasn't sure which towel was having the tougher time. Adrian was so thin that his towel seemed desperate for something to grasp. Butch had the opposite problem. His towel was having a tough time staying closed around his burgeoning waistline.

Adrian cupped his hands and shouted to Al. "Can you hear me?"

"Yes," Al shouted back. "Can you hear me?"

"Yup," said Adrian.

"Loud and clear," Butch snarled.

"Okay then, just like we agreed. Each of you get in your diving position, and when you are ready, say, 'Okay.' I'll count to three and say, 'Go,' and you are off, right?"

Both men gestured their approval. Each of them took a few moments to find a comfortable place upon which to perch. When they both seemed to be ready, they were only inches away from each other. Signifying they were both ready, both men whipped off their towels. Al cringed, silently pleading that the park be as empty as it seemed. Giving two naked middle-aged men the right to swim the Delaware in the middle of the night was probably not what George Washington and his men thought they were fighting a revolution for.

After a naked eternity, Adrian shouted, "Okay," and Butch followed suit. Al took a breath.

"Okay! One, two, three, go!" he shouted quickly, so as to get the men in the water as soon as possible. They both seemed to be momentarily startled at Al's quick count, but they dived in full bore. Adrian's was the more graceful dive, but Butch's push-off was more powerful and he got off to an early lead, his arms buzz-sawing through the current. He quickly opened a full-body-length lead on Adrian, then a second body length. Al watched, concerned, as this was not what Adrian promised would happen. Al shot a nervous glance around the parking lot, expecting at any moment to encounter an investigative reporter wondering why he was so interested in watching two naked men swim at four in the morning.

Butch reached the halfway point in the river and continued plowing forward. When Adrian reached the halfway point, about ten seconds later, the race suddenly changed. Adrian shifted into high gear, his arms beating through the water like an overcaffeinated beaver. Within a few seconds, Adrian pulled even with, and then ahead of, the tiring Butch. Twenty feet to go and Adrian pulled well ahead. Closing in on the shoreline . . . ten feet to go . . . five feet . . . Adrian hit the shoreline and pulled himself out of the water, giddy with victory.

"Yeah! That's what I'm talking about!" Adrian shouted, dancing a nakedly uninhibited victory jig. Watching this was not Al's idea of an inspired evening.

"Adrian! Stop flinging around!" Al shouted.

"Hey! I earned the right to fling it around! You see that victory?"

"I'm seeing a lot more than I ever wanted to see! Get dressed!"

Adrian turned to the river. Butch was struggling to finish. He was close to the shoreline, but he was swimming in slow motion. Finally, Butch reached the banking shoreline and started to pull himself out of the river. Adrian watched with smug satisfaction as the burly bartender pulled his head out of the water and got up on one knee, gasping for air.

"Welcome to New Jersey!" Adrian shouted at Butch. "Glad you could make it!"

Butch responded with a river of obscenities that were impossible to understand between his deep gasps for air.

"Get in the car!" Adrian shouted through cupped hands to Al. They both began running as Butch tried to steady himself on his exhausted legs. Both men rushed to the car and slipped in through the already-open doors.

"Drive!" Adrian shouted as he slammed his door.

"Your clothes are in the back!" Al said, shutting his door. "Please get dressed."

"Go!" Adrian shouted again.

"We're going to leave him?"

"Too slow on the uptake, Al! Yes! Go!"

Butch was now approaching them, panting and gasping. Having watched the two of them dash for the car, he knew something was fishy.

"Hey!" he gasped. "You wait up for me!" He began waving his arms and shouting. "Hey!"

"There's a naked man running at us!" Adrian shouted, feigning shock, then breaking out into a silly high-pitched laugh at the sight of Butch in the headlights. The narrow beams of light and encroaching shadows made Butch's flailing arms seem more exaggerated. Just as Butch reached the front hood of the car, Al threw the vehicle into reverse and hit the gas pedal hard. The car screeched backward and Butch fell over.

"Should we throw him his clothes?" Al asked.

"Will you just go!" Adrian implored him. Al threw the car into drive, turned it, and sped away, up the steep roadway and out of the park.

"I don't get it, Adrian!" Al shouted over the motor as he

continued to press on the gas pedal. "What did we accomplish?"

Meanwhile, Butch, his lungs still screaming for air, picked himself up and watched the car speed away.

"Stop!" he half-shouted, half-rasped, between breaths. Figuring it was better for him to save his breath, he began running as fast as his cramping middle-aged legs would carry him. The car was up the hill and out of the park in no time, but Butch was determined to keep after it. "I don't care where you go!" he shouted. "I'll find you, you son of a—"

Suddenly a bright circle of light scooted across Butch's face. It was a flashlight. The ambient light revealed the holder was wearing the dark brown shirt and distinctive hat of a park-service ranger.

"What have we here?" asked the ranger. "Lady Godiva's husband?"

Al wasn't sure how much time had passed, but he had learned his lesson and wasn't going to ask. He and Adrian now stood in front of the local courthouse, a restoration of white marble nineteenth-century Roman architecture, with magnificent pillars holding up the front portico.

"Let me ask you something, Adrian. Did you beat Lowe fair and square? Were you that good a swimmer?"

"What are you implying?" Adrian asked self-righteously.

"You cut through the water like an outboard motor. You were going impossibly fast."

"One thing you will learn in heaven, Al. There are no random or independent acts. Everything that must happen, will happen, and it is all related."

"Okay, but you didn't answer my question."

"Yes," Adrian replied. "I did. You'll see soon enough. Come on. It's time." Adrian made his way up the steps of the courthouse with Al in pursuit.

"Time for what?" Al asked, shouting ahead. "I thought you said time was meaningless!"

Adrian stopped, turned, and gave his partner an exasperated look.

"Al . . . we're on earth now." He shook his head and opened the door of the courthouse. "You've got to get faster on the uptake."

Al bit his tongue and walked past Adrian into the building. Adrian walked them down a narrow corridor, stopping in front of Courtroom Number 1. There was a square window in the door, about eye-high, which allowed them to see the proceeding inside. A chastened and fully clothed Butch Lowe was standing in front of the judge's bench, hands clasped behind his back, head bowed. An attorney stood at his side.

"Shall we?" Adrian said, and softly opened the door. Al and Adrian entered as the judge was speaking.

"Only because of your past reputation as a swimming champion in this area do you get a pass on the charges brought by the park service," the judge chided. "But as for the rest . . . the defendant has admitted his culpability on the charge of indecent exposure and cre-ating a public nuisance. The court finds that the defendant's plea of guilty is acceptable and warranted. Hiram Lowe, I sentence you to pay a fine, including court costs, of five hundred and forty dollars." The judge rapped the gavel, indicating the end of the proceeding.

Al looked over at Adrian.

"That's a familiar number," Al said.

"It's what he took from you on the paper route. Consider resti-tution complete," Adrian said. As they spoke, Butch noticed their presence in the back of the room. Butch whispered something to his attorney, then turned and headed down the aisle directly toward them. The attorney made a valiant try to restrain his client, but Butch would not be deterred.

"Butch!" Adrian said softly. "Good to see you dry and dressed! Last time I saw you, you were floundering around on the Delaware River shore. I thought you were Flipper in heat!"

Somehow, Butch maintained his control.

"I don't know who you boys are or why you picked on me," he said through gritted teeth, "but I'll be sure to see you around. Why don't you come back to the Gnarled Limb tonight?"

"Sorry, can't." Adrian smiled and walked backward toward the door. "We're going swimming in my father's pool. You know . . . the nice heated one." Adrian slipped through the door, holding it open for Al, who followed but then stuck his head back into the court-room. This time Al had no trouble looking Butch right in the eye.

"Who loves ya, baby?" he blurted out, and shut the door.

The click of recognition went off in Butch's head. He swung the door open violently and stormed down the corridor. He'd catch them in the lobby; no way the punk whose paper-route money he used to take was going to get away with this. When Butch reached the lobby, he was surprised to find it empty. "They could not have moved that fast," he thought. His attorney called for him to cool off, but Butch ignored him and headed for the door, punched it open, and stepped onto the portico. There was no one there.

CHAPTER 12

the second jerk al mitchell
meets on earth

THE SWIRLING MIST enveloped Al and although he had no sensation of floating or movement, he could see Adrian partially through the swirls and he was sure they were no longer at the courthouse.

"Did you see how Butch looked when he recognized me?" Al shouted, obviously pleased. "How about the way that shriveled old bastard ran after us? I thought he was going to sock you right in the jaw when you told him you had three swimming championships and he had two!" Al was obviously pumped, and Adrian enjoyed the rare show of enthusiasm from his companion.

"That was a very angry man we saw in New Hope," Adrian

intoned seriously, then grinned. "In fact, we saw more of him than we ever should have!"

By the time both men stopped laughing, they were sitting again. The thick mist made it impossible to see exactly where he was, but one thing Al knew for certain—he wasn't sitting in the spongy old theater chair. This seat was rock hard and unforgiving.

The first wisps of the mist cleared, revealing his seat to be a beautifully polished white marble bench, armless, its back arched over like a curling ocean wave. A bit more of the mist cleared and Al could make out Adrian sitting on the bench with him.

"Where are we?" Al asked, but Adrian sat mute, indicating with a broad sweep of his hand that Al should look for himself and see. Al waved away some of the mist in front of his face and began to make out a wall not far behind him. It was made of sandstone and mortar, was laid out with the same geometric precision as the pyramids, and went as high as the eye could see. There were hieroglyphics and small carved figures on the wall. Al stood up to get a better look at the figures, but before he could focus on them, the lingering mist dissipated all at once, revealing the wall as part of a cavernous room of breathtaking proportions and design. The rectangular room was so massive and long, Al could barely make out the far end of it.

"Oh, my God," Al said, his mouth hanging open in awe. "What is this place?" He deliberately spoke in a muted tone. Even with his jaded view of everything, Al recognized the regal bearing of this room and he innately understood it commanded respect and reverence. He marveled at the wonders surrounding him—dozens of huge ornately designed pillars reaching from the floor like the fingers of a mythic god to support a ceiling at least five stories high; an inlaid tile floor patterned in a multicolor swirl that led the eye to an elliptical reflecting pool in the middle of the room, the pool surrounded by a phalanx of lush green potted plants. There were statues and busts everywhere: bearded muscular men, some in togas, some naked—thinkers, orators, warriors, in classic ancient poses; also animals whose final fate must have been with an expert taxidermist—birds, jackals, cats, wolves, dogs, in full-color lifelike poses.

"Close your mouth, Al," Adrian said bemusedly. "This is the Library of Alexandria in ancient Egypt. We mentioned it before, so I thought you'd like to see it."

"I didn't think they could build something this incredible so long ago," Al said, finally clamping his jaw shut.

"It should have been one of the wonders of the ancient world," Adrian continued. "Alexandria was an amazing city at this time. It was the second city in the Roman Empire after Rome itself—sort of the way Chicago is to New York City. The Egyptians accumulated almost all the world's knowledge at the time in this one place—some say over four hundred thousand scrolls and volumes at its peak." Adrian pointed down the length of the room. "If you look, you can see many doors leading out of this room. They lead to classrooms, auditoriums, lecture halls . . . just like a university. Scholars, mathematicians, scientists, philosophers, did their reading and thinking here for hundreds of years."

As Adrian spoke, Al made his way over to the nearby wall to study the carvings. The sandstone and mortar were in excellent shape, as though the room were new. The hieroglyphics, punctuated occasionally by long narrow slits that allowed in both air and sunlight, were crisp, precise, and incredibly detailed. In the first set of drawings Al studied, five men sat shoulder to shoulder, cross-legged, each scooping and eating something from a bowl nestled in his lap. In a second set of carvings directly below these, the men were engaged in athletic contests, one throwing a discus, another a javelin, a third was in a full sprint with a laurel wreath wrapped around his forehead, and the remaining two were locked in a wrestling hold, surrounded by rooting spectators.

"What would you call this?" Al asked, rubbing his finger over the carved figures. "ESPN B.C.?"

Adrian peered over and studied the athletic figures a moment.

"Maybe they are posing for Egyptian Wheaties boxes," he quipped.

"They didn't have Wheaties back then," Al said, walking back to the bench. "Just Sugar Frosted Pharaohs."

Adrian pulled out his HEAVEN box again. "Who is the next jerk for us to HARP on?"

Al looked a bit wistful as he sat down.

"This one's from my college years. A girl named Morgan Telford."

Adrian nodded and repeated the name into the device. The machine whirred and purred for a few moments. Adrian brightened.

"Hey, looks like you're two for two, Al! She's still on earth. We got a read on her! This should be interesting." Adrian closed the HEAVEN box. "Don't get up while this is going on."

"While what's—" Before Al could finish his question, a trumpet fanfare echoed through the great room, followed by a slow but faint drumbeat. Two columns of ancient Egyptian soldiers appeared at the far end of the library, small at first, as if they were very far away, then, as they got closer and larger, the pounding of the drums increased. There were ten soldiers in each column as they marched solemnly past the myriad statues and the reflecting pool, coming to a halt in front of the bench. The drums went silent as from between the columns of soldiers appeared a husky, white-robed man wearing a vibrant blue-and-yellow headdress almost as tall as he was.

"That's one of their high priests," Adrian whispered.

"I thought it was Yul Brynner," Al said as he watched the priest remove the ungainly headdress and set it on the floor. "What's with the hat? He could hide King Tut in that thing."

The priest wiped his bald head, then stood absolutely still. Adrian stifled a giggle. "What's funny now?" Al asked.

"You know what you could call Tut's pyramid?" Adrian whispered to Al. "Tut's hut. Or you could call his backside Tut's butt."

"Don't start this stupid stuff again," Al whispered back. They both stared at the motionless priest. Al knew he wasn't going to be able to help himself. He turned to Adrian. "What do you call his stomach?"

"Tut's gut." Adrian nodded. "How about his dog?"

Al thought for a moment. "Tut's mutt."

"Right. Now listen."

The priest produced a papyrus from the golden sash holding his robe at the waist, looked up, and called out in a ringing baritone, "Morgan Telford!"

The drums started again, this time with a more modern, up-tempo beat to keep pace with the sashaying holograph of the shapely young lady who was making her way between the columns of soldiers, past the high priest, and onto the library floor. She was perfectly manicured in her lime-colored designer dress and pumps, which accented her large green eyes. Her short blonde hair fell in pointed bangs on her forehead as though pointing with relish at what Al once called her "kick-ass" smile. She took up a pose in front of the boys, giving them a chin-down, eyes-up "peekaboo" stare that to the casual observer looked cute, but to the seasoned observer, such as Al, was very calculated.

"Honored guests," the high priest resumed as if chanting a prayer, "let us meet our second subject. She was born in Bristol, Connecticut, at the start of the first year of her life. She moved to New Jersey at the age of ten. As a child and teenager, she entered many beauty contests only to win first runner-up in the Miss New Jersey Tuna Casserole Pageant."

"She did make a great tuna fish casserole." Al nodded. "It was my favorite."

The high priest continued. "Following twelve years of nondescript academic performance in grade school and high school, Morgan became a regular member of the dean's list in college!"

"Her grade point average increased with her bust size," Al said.

"She is now known as Mrs. Morgan Ann Telford Olson." As the bald man continued, the image of the young Morgan melted into a more mature, middle-aged woman. Al watched the changeover and was still impressed with her looks—it was either healthy habits or a great plastic surgeon. "She married Dr. Prescott Olson, a successful orthopedic surgeon, in 1991. They have no children. They travel frequently and have an apartment on Park Avenue in New York City, a vacation home in Maine, and a condominium in Aspen, Colorado, for their annual skiing vacation."

Adrian gave Morgan the once-over and nodded approvingly. "I wouldn't mind skiing down her peaks myself."

Now it was Al's turn to give Adrian the once-over.

"Are you sure you're an angel?" Al asked.

"What would make you ask that?" Adrian snapped.

"No big deal." Al shrugged.

"Sure it's a big deal." Adrian whacked him on the arm. "Otherwise you wouldn't have brought it up. Why did you ask if I'm an angel?"

"It's just that . . ." Al trailed off reluctantly.

"Go ahead, say it!" Adrian demanded.

"Remember I said you seemed more like a stand-up comic than an angel? Maybe I was wrong. You seem more like a frat boy than an angel."

"Why?" Adrian jumped off the bench. "Because I'm not floating around with a little harp under my chin singing 'Hosanna' with the heavenly chorus?" Adrian was fully animated now. Al had obviously pushed his button. "Do you know how long the waiting list is to get on the heavenly chorus? Forget it! They stopped taking names for it in the sixteenth century."

"It's not just that. . . . It's the way you look."

"How am I supposed to look?"

"Where are your wings, for instance?"

Adrian rolled his eyes in disgust."Wings!" he muttered to himself, his look betraying a here-we-go-again attitude. "Come on, Al! Wings are so medieval! I thought you were beyond that!" As Adrian ranted, his face turned redder, his voice higher in pitch. "You have to get faster on the uptake, Al! Did you ever stop to think how aerodynamically impractical wings are? To support body weight, wings would have to weigh more than the back could tolerate. You'd be a hunchback. And you'd have to exercise the wings every day to keep them strong. Did you ever think of that?

Can you imagine Richard Simmons doing wing-exercise videos?"

Adrian began flapping his arms like an uncoordinated bird, his voice imitating the exercise guru. "Come on, everybody. Work those wings! One time up . . . one time down. . . . Sing 'Locomotion' as we go. . . . 'Everybody's doin' a brand-new dance now / (C'mon, baby, do the loco-motion)'!"

Al grabbed Adrian's arm.

"Take it easy, Adrian," he said calmly.

Adrian blinked a few times, as though he didn't know where he was, then stopped. He quickly recovered his composure. "Sorry. This is a sore point with me."

"I couldn't tell," Al said softly.

"I'll explain why some other time."

"Okay, Adrian. Forget about the wings. How about we get back to Morgan Telford?"

"Good idea." Adrian took a deep breath. "Tell me why you have a beef with Morgan Telford."

"I met Morgan my sophomore year in college," Al said sheepishly. "We were both in Algebra Two. We hit it off very well . . . I mean *very* well! At least I thought we did. For the next few months we had a pretty hot affair going. I stayed in her dorm a lot; we took weekend trips together. All the while, I'm doing the course work and the homework for the both of us. I even figured out a signaling system to give her answers on tests. Needless to say, we both passed the course easily. In fact, we both made the dean's list. To celebrate, I set up a weekend in Vermont just before Christmas. I'm thinking the Ward Cleaver thing is in our future . . . a house, two kids, a mortgage. So, I figure I'd spring the big ring on her while we were in Vermont. The night before the trip . . .

December 1979

Al leaned over the jewelry case to get one more look at the diamond rock reflecting back the display-counter light in a rainbow of colors. The woman behind the counter assured him it was a quality diamond, handsomely mounted. He was taken aback at the price, but, what the hell, it was Christmas! Al opened a charge account at the store and bought the ring. Over the next few hours he swept up a diamond watch, some blouses and a turtleneck, fuzzy slippers, and a musical jewelry box.

Darkness had come and a tired Al kicked open the door to his one-room apartment and somehow squeezed through with the shopping bags piled in his arms. He'd barely made it across the room to his bed, when the bags came crashing down. He peeked out the window at the foot of his bed to enjoy the Christmas-light displays bathing his dark room in a multitude of colors. This was as good as Al could feel. This was going to be the special weekend! If all went right, Saturday night would be the ring. It couldn't be any better! Al flipped on the light and made his way to the tiny refrigerator and pulled out a can of beer. He opened it and began slurping it down, then noticed the blinking light on his answering machine.

"Hey, Al," the first message began, "Ronnie here. Next Tuesday, intramural basketball begins. We have the gym at seven P.M. for practice, seven-thirty for the

game. I'm assuming you'll be there. No need to get back to me, unless you are not going to make it." The first message clicked off.

"Sounds good," Al replied to the machine as he finished the beer, then, in his best NBA jump-shot style, flung the empty beer can through the air and directly into the garbage bin. Al raised his arms in mock triumph. The triumph lasted only a few seconds more.

The second message began to play.

"Hey, Al, honey. This is Morgan." Her voice sounded uncharacteristically hesitant. *"Listen, honey, some-thing's come up. I can't go to Vermont this weekend. In fact, a lot of things have come up . . . so many things I don't even know where to start. But the fact of the matter is, I think we should back off and not see so much of each other. You know what I mean? I'm not ready to go into a really serious relationship right now. I know you were counting on this weekend a lot, and I should have told you earlier . . . but . . . I didn't want to . . . disappoint you too much."* She sighed. *"I don't know how much time I have left on this stupid machine, so let me wrap it up. You are a great guy, Al, you really were great to be around and I enjoyed it. But I'm going to move on and I think you should, too. I'm sure I'll see you next semester after the holidays and we can talk."* She paused again. *"Bye for now . . . and . . . Merry Chris—"* The message clicked off.

Al was standing confrontationally in front of Morgan's holograph.

"I probably replayed that message twenty times that night," he said bitterly, then sat down. "Who knows how many more times that weekend? I'd never been let down so badly before in my life."

"She can't hear you, Al," Adrian said sympathetically.

"Broke my heart," Al said to her face: "First time and last I ever let that happen," he said to no one in particular. Al shifted his numbing butt on the marble bench. "There is more to the story. A couple of weeks into the next semester I met this guy in my history class. Guess what? The year before, he had been in Morgan's physical science class. He did the same thing . . . hot and heavy romance . . . all the while he's doing all the course work for both of them. When the semester ends, she makes the dean's list and he makes the chump's list. Morgan dumped him the next day."

"I see," Adrian said. "Instead of a gold digger, we've got a grade digger."

Al straightened up with a bolt of energy and began rubbing his hands together. "What are we going to do to her?"

"Let's see what we can come up with." Adrian studied his HEAVEN box intently. "You want to guess what she is doing now?"

"I bet she is doing missionary work on an uncharted island in the South Pacific."

"You're pretty close," Adrian lied. "She's a New York City socialite. She throws parties. She attends fund-raisers. She reads every fashion magazine in the world. And, more than anything else in the world, she shops . . . every day on Fifth Avenue."

"So, what do we do to a world champion shopper?" Al pondered. "Revoke her credit card? Lock her out of Macy's white sale? Scramble the Home Shopping Network satellite feed?"

Adrian continued to thoughtfully study his HEAVEN box. Finally he lit up.

"I think I found it! You ever hear of the New York Art Institute? It's a very prestigious organization." Adrian generated that sly smile once again. "Come on. We have work to do."

⌒ Mrs. Morgan Telford Olson emerged from her Park Avenue building in a salmon-colored skirt and jacket and was escorted to her waiting car by a broad-shouldered doorman.

"Have a nice day, Mrs. Olson," the doorman said as she brushed by him and into the back of the car.

"You, too," she replied brusquely as he shut the car door. She took out her electronic planner and began scanning the screen. "I need to go to the art institute building and then to the loft in SoHo," she called out to her driver without looking up. Giving it his best the customer-is-always-right smile, Adrian turned from behind the wheel and tipped his chauffeur's cap.

"Good morning, Mrs. Olson. My name is Adrian." The unfamiliar voice made Morgan looked up.

"Where is Mohammar?" she asked impatiently.

"He's sick today, ma'am. But don't worry"—Adrian kicked the limo into drive—"I know my way around the city. I hope you don't mind that I brought along one of our trainee drivers as well." Al turned quickly and nodded, trying to get a measure of the woman this many years later without giving her the chance to recognize him. Not to worry as it turned out, because Morgan was much more interested in her ringing cell phone.

"Chloe? Morning, girl," she said into the phone. "I'm heading over to pick up my painting right now. Klaus finished it overnight.

. . . Yes . . . he complained all week I was rushing him . . . but I made it worth his while if you know what I mean." She giggled into the phone. "I have to give the painting to those dried-up old toads when I meet them at three o'clock. I'm not being harsh. . . . I don't give a damn about them or the stupid painting, but I do give a damn about getting on the board . . . because I am getting tired of life in the Big Apple. . . . I hate the winters." She lowered her voice. "There is a big-shot Hollywood producer on the board. He's getting divorced. If I can hook up with him . . . who knows? I wouldn't mind moving to Tinseltown." This time her laugh resembled an evil cackle. "No, I haven't said anything to Preston!" she said as though the answer should have been obvious. "Girl, if I'm going to move to California, I'm not taking Mr. Formaldehyde with me, count on that." She lowered her voice again, but not low enough where Adrian and Al could not hear her. "I'm not going to say anything to him. You know me . . . the siren of surprise! If I go, I'll leave him a message on our answering machine. You know how good I am at that."

Hearing that last sentence, Al began biting his lip—hard. He was steamed. He watched as Adrian pulled the car to the curb in front of the New York Art Institute building, an imposing structure set back off the street at the top of a double flight of stone steps.

"Listen, girl," Morgan said, noticing where they were, "I have to go." She slipped the phone back into her purse. Adrian turned the car off and nudged Al.

"Get out and open the door for her," he whispered, but Al responded with an are-you-crazy look, and, with as much forcefulness as he could muster in a whisper, said, "She can stick the door up her—"

"Coming, Mrs. Olson," Adrian said politely as he shot out and rushed around to open the back passenger door. Morgan got out and gave him a playful smile.

"You sure are a hell of a lot faster than Mohammar!" she deftly ran her finger under Adrian's chin. "Sometimes, it's good to be fast." She smiled suggestively. "Other times, it's better to go slow and take your time, don't you think?"

"Whatever you say, Mrs. Olson," Adrian replied matter-of-factly. Knowing what Morgan had done to Al, Adrian had taken an immediate and deep dislike to the woman. He was hoping it didn't show.

"Wait here." she winked. "I should be back in about ten minutes." As she walked away, Adrian wiped with distaste at the part of his face she had touched. Al got out of the car and leaned against it as he watched her walk up the stairs to the institute.

"I'll leave him a message on our answering machine. You know how good I am at that!" he imitated her less than flatteringly as she disappeared into the building. "Boy, I wish she was a tennis ball and I was Venus Williams's racket." He looked up at Adrian. "Why are we at the art institute?"

"Very simple. There's an opening on the art institute's board of directors and because Mr. Formaldehyde, as she calls her husband, contributes so much to the institute, Morgan is a finalist for the seat."

"And you're planning on stopping her?" Al asked. "What are you going to do? Take her for a swim in the Delaware River?"

"No, not quite." Adrian laughed. "There is a law against polluting rivers."

"What, then?"

"The New York Art Institute was founded about forty years ago by a couple of philanthropists, Merriman and Eliza Tomlinson," Adrian explained. "The Tomlinsons are very old now, but they still appoint all board members directly. And they have a very unique way of doing it, and that is where out chance lies."

"Here she comes!" Al interrupted Adrian.

"That was fast," Adrian said.

"Believe me, this woman works fast," Al said, opening his door. "You let her in." As Al got in the car, Morgan stopped in front of Adrian, leaving only a sliver of space between them.

"We need to get to the loft right away," she said. "You know where the loft is?"

"Yes, ma'am." Adrian tipped his cap. "Mohammar told me everything."

"Oh God, I hope he didn't tell you *everything*." Morgan exaggerated the last word, feigning shock, and running her hand up and down his tie. "Or at least if he did, I hope you won't think less of me." Morgan flashed a lot of leg at him as she slithered into the backseat. Adrian gave her a nod and shut the door. As soon as he turned away, Adrian's face soured.

"Don't worry, Mrs. Olson," he said softly. "I couldn't possibly think any less of you."

℮ The limo whisked through the business district in midtown Manhattan and into a section of the city called SoHo, where struggling artists and actors sit in closet-sized coffee bars by day and avant-garde theaters by night, sharing poetry, musings, cramped studio apartments, and converted warehouse lofts as they await their big break.

Adrian pulled in front of a particularly old warehouse, one that had been recently refurbished with fine oak touches, but that retained many characteristics of its original use. It had double front doors, which, when both were opened, were tall and wide enough to allow in a large truck. It had originally been built without windows, so new sashes and frames had been installed on both sides of the frontage. There were windows on both sides of the doors, at street level and at the second level, indicating two apartments on each of those floors. The windows on the third floor ran the width of the building, suggesting the third floor was a single loft. Adrian double-parked the limo in front of the warehouse, alongside a Volkswagen and an overflowing garbage bin.

"Adrian, why doesn't . . ." Morgan hesitated and leaned forward. "I'm sorry, I forgot your name," she said to Al.

"Alberto," Al responded without turning around.

"Of course, Alberto. Why don't you wait here in case the police turn up and want the car moved." Morgan began to get out of the car. "Adrian, you come upstairs with me. I'm going to need you to carry something for me."

Adrian gave Al the same all-knowing wink he had given him while they were sitting at Butch Lowe's bar. He joined Morgan on the sidewalk and followed her through the oversized front doors, which she opened automatically with a card key. They walked through a stuffy narrow hallway and onto a steamy elevator. Morgan stood directly in front of the control panel as the doors closed. Adrian waited a few moments for her to push the button to the second floor, but when she didn't, he reached around her to do it himself. She deliberately blocked his arm.

"Sorry," he said to her. "I thought we wanted to go up."

"We do." She turned to him with her most sultry look. "What's your hurry? Don't you think being trapped on an elevator is sexy?"

"I think being trapped on an elevator has its ups and downs." Adrian smirked, thrusting his arm toward the control panel again only to have Morgan grab it and pull it around her waist.

"Reminds me of the movie *Fatal Attraction*!" she purred, running her hand up and down a reluctant Adrian's back. "Remember what Glenn Close did to Michael Douglas on the elevator?"

"I remember what Glenn Close did to the rabbit in the stew pot," Adrian replied, wedging his left arm between them and pulling free. This time he pressed the button emphatically, and the elevator motor hummed to life. As the car began to slowly lift, Morgan backed off and threw her hands on her hips.

"I thought Mohammar told you all about me," she said.

"He told me all I need to know," Adrian replied dryly.

"So, what's the matter? You gay?"

"Nope," Adrian replied as the elevator stopped and the doors opened. "It's just that I don't fool around on the job."

"Oh, I get it." Morgan smiled pointedly, walking past him and out the doors. "You're too good for stuff like this. You're an angel."

For the first time, Adrian brightened.

"You could say that."

℃ Adrian followed Morgan to the end of the second-floor hallway and up a spiral staircase to a windowless vestibule on the third floor. There was a bright red door directly in front of them and Morgan pressed the doorbell next to it, once, then a second time impatiently. A flustered voice called "Hold on, hold on" from the other side of the door. Finally, it opened and out stepped a little man with a pointy nose, a similarly pointed beard, and beetlelike eyes. He wore a paint-smeared smock.

"Hello, Klaus." Morgan beamed her best smile as they embraced and kissed passionately.

"It is done," Klaus proclaimed as if announcing a major world event. "I put the final touches on this morning." Klaus pushed the door open and escorted Morgan inside. As Adrian took a step to follow, Klaus lightly touched his arm and shook his head.

Seeing this, Morgan sauntered back over to Adrian and smiled.

"You wait here," she said cattily. "Klaus and I have some business to transact." Klaus raised his eyebrows in response and escorted Morgan back through the door.

"How long should I wait, ma'am?" Adrian said in his best professional voice. Morgan looked back.

"I won't be long. I'm just going to boil me a rabbit." The door slammed shut.

Adrian heard the hum of the elevator, its doors open, then after a few silent moments, the clang of shoes on the metal of the spiral staircase. Al appeared, winding himself up the steps, then stepping into the vestibule.

"I got a parking spot, so I thought I'd come up," he explained.

"Somebody needs to hose that Morgan down," Adrian said, shaking his head.

"Where is she?"

"She's inside with her artist friend. I'm supposed to wait until I'm summoned."

"Why don't you finish telling me what we're doing here."

Adrian began pacing.

"Okay, Al, stay on the uptake with me. Morgan wants the open seat on the art institute's board of directors, right? The original founders of the art institute, the Tomlinsons, have a unique way of picking board members. The Tomlinsons only want art lovers on their board. They judge candidates based on their artistic expression. So every candidate for the board has to create his or her own original painting or photo or other work of art to represent their personal artistic expression."

"But Morgan's no artist . . . or art lover," Al said disgustedly. "She couldn't draw a stick figure if you gave her a head start by drawing the stick!"

"Which is why she hired ol' Klaus here to paint for her. She's going to represent his painting as her own to the Tomlinsons at a meeting she has with them this afternoon." Suddenly the door swung open and a slightly disheveled Morgan poked her smiling face into the vestibule. "Oh, Alberto! You're here now, too! Good! You boys can come in now." Morgan brushed out the wrinkles in her salmon outfit as she led Al and Adrian through a long hallway and into Klaus's loft, a spacious domed room that functioned mostly as his studio. There were easels and canvases standing and stacked in various parts of the room, paint smears on the nearby walls and floor. In a far nook was the living space, which was nothing more than a small kitchenette, a chair, and a rumpled bed. Klaus was standing in the middle of the room, beaming at a particular painting. He turned it toward Morgan so she could see it as she approached. It was a still life of white and pink lilies sprouting around a green moss-encrusted pond.

"What do you think?" he asked smugly, confident of the answer.

"He's going to pull a muscle patting himself on the back," Al whispered to Adrian.

"Nice," Morgan said flatly, "should do the trick."

"Nice? Do the trick? This is all you can say?" Klaus shouted resentfully.

"I told you, I'm no art connoisseur." Morgan laughed. "I said it looks good . . . fine. However you want me to describe it, is how I'll describe it."

Klaus snorted, then took Morgan into his arms again and gave her a long kiss. He then pushed her away dramatically, his eyes bulging. "Your diffidence shall not weather my enthusiasm. Your approbation is my motivation and my inspiration!" he shouted melodramatically, thrusting his paintbrush in the air.

"He sounds like Gomez Addams," Al whispered. "Next thing you know he's going to start kissing her up her arm."

"If he does, ring for Lurch," said Adrian.

"I am told Mrs. Tomlinson loves lilies," Klaus said, snaking his arms around Morgan's waist. "Thus, here you have a pool of them." Klaus traced the lilies with his fingers as he spoke. "Say to her that lilies are soft, beautiful, and harbingers of the sweet smells and sights of spring! The very characteristics you think of when you think of Eliza Tomlinson!"

"Now, that I like!" Morgan beamed. "That's exactly what I will tell her!" She pulled Klaus's face close to hers. "As soon as I get on the board, we will have an exhibit of new artists and you will be first!" They kissed again.

"I think I'm going to barf," Al said under his breath as Morgan turned to Adrian.

"I need you to carefully wrap up this painting and bring it down to the car," she said.

"There is a cloth cover over there." Klaus pointed dismissively to a spot near the bed. Adrian grabbed it and approached the canvas. As he began draping the cloth over the painting, Morgan sauntered over to him.

"You and Alberto take it down to the car and wait for me. I'll be a few more minutes up here." She gave Adrian that you-know-why smile. "Unless you want me to have Klaus take the painting down to the car with Alberto and you can stay up here with me."

Adrian finished covering the painting. "Alberto and I will be in the car."

"Suit yourself." Morgan pouted as an annoyed Klaus walked over and grabbed her arm.

"You should go now," he said firmly to both men. Al grabbed one end of the painting and helped Adrian negotiate it through the narrow hallway toward the door. They tried to ignore the heavy breathing and the giggling they could hear coming from the loft.

"Sounds like Klaus is getting paid in full," Adrian said.

"Yeah," Al said, "but if I were him, I wouldn't listen to my answering machine tonight."

The Tomlinson estate covered twenty acres in the Hamptons on Long Island. It was everything an old-money estate should be, beginning with the pair of wrought iron gates at the head of the driveway, each adorned with a gold-scripted *T*. The gates connected to a precisely manicured hedgerow that surrounded the entire estate and hid the security fence protecting the rest of the property.

"Mrs. Morgan Telford Olson to see Mr. and Mrs. Tomlinson," Adrian shouted from the driver's side window into a loudspeaker planted in front of the gates.

"Thank you," replied a faceless security voice.

"Order me a Big Mac and fries while you are at it," Al said.

The gates glided open and Adrian slowly brought the car up the tree-lined driveway, stopping in the roundabout fronting the red-brick colonial mansion. A pair of stiff-backed butlers in black slacks and white coats stood waiting on the small circular porch. One stepped quickly off the porch and opened the car door for Morgan.

"Welcome, Mrs. Olson." he held out his hand to help her out of the car. "Mr. and Mrs. Tomlinson are so looking forward to meeting you."

"Thank you," Morgan said with a bit of dramatic flair as she stepped from the limo.

"If you will be so kind as to follow Raymond into the parlor," he said obsequiously, pointing to the butler still standing on the porch, "he will get you some refreshment. I will help get your painting set up in the sunroom where Mr. and Mrs. Tomlinson can better see it and appreciate it."

"Of course." Morgan turned to Adrian, who had gotten out of the car. "You will see to the painting, won't you Adrian, dear?"

"You bet I will," Adrian replied.

Adrian and Al followed the butler around the side of the mansion and through a side door into the Tomlinsons' glass-encased conservatory. With the exception of a square table in the center of the room displaying a silver tea setting for four, the room was empty. The butler retrieved an easel from a corner and set it up near the table. Adrian set the painting on it gently, the cloth covering still intact. The butler checked the positioning of the painting against the sunlight flooding into the room.

"Good," he said. "Mr. and Mrs. Tomlinson cannot see very well these days. The daylight in this room helps them a lot."

"Maybe we could drive the car around and shine the headlights through the glass if that would help," Al joked. The butler turned to him, unamused.

"Mr. Tomlinson did not amass his fortune by suffering fools gladly or by wasting time learning a sense of humor. You two can let yourselves out the door you entered." With that, the butler exited through a different door into the mansion.

"I guess I'm feeling pretty rebuked," Al said.

"Forget about it." Adrian laughed and grabbed the painting off the easel. "We have to work fast."

℘ The mist surrounded them in an instant, and just as quickly it was gone. Al and Adrian were standing on an outside balcony perched on the second floor of a gently rounded stucco building. Below them was a chaotic street scene of people in medieval garb squeezing past one another on foot or on horseback, each trying to wind their way past vendors, beggars, and the hundreds of cows and other barnyard animals milling about freely. Modest homes and shops built of straw or wood lined both sides of the street, which sloped gently downward, ending in front of a white church, its steeple rising high above any other building in sight. Behind the church, and stretching in either direction, lay an open sandy beach and the vista of a crystalline blue sea. After admiring the scene for a few moments, Adrian turned to Al.

"Do you know where we are?" he asked.

"Looks like we're in the Mediterranean somewhere . . . maybe Italy?"

"Very good." Adrian nodded. "We're in Florence . . . at least a heavenly re-creation of Florence during the Renaissance."

"What's it re-created for?"

"For the master." Adrian pointed to the doorway behind them, which led from the portico into the stucco building.

"What master?"

As if on cue, a sullen-looking, round-shouldered man with a chest-length beard and long straggly white hair walked through the doorway and onto the portico. He was fairly broad shouldered and heavyset, but he moved gracefully. He wore an overlong pullover top and a leather cap drawn low on his forehead from under which shone eyes as blue as the Mediterranean.

"Hello, Master," Adrian said respectfully and a bit nervously.

"I am told you are in need of my talent," the old man rasped, rubbing his darkly tanned face.

"Yes. It is a small matter in relation to your talent."

"You need from me a painting?"

"Yes," Adrian replied, but before he could continue, the old man walked back into the building. Al was pretty sure he recognized the man's face from textbooks he had seen.

"Was that . . ." he hesitated a moment, "Leonardo da Vinci?"

"It's not Leonardo DiCaprio," Adrian responded. Al was impressed again.

"That's da Vinci, huh?"

"Don't call him by his name. Call him Master. That's the title he likes."

"What's in there?" Al asked, peering through the doorway.

"His studio," Adrian replied. "He's like a one-man Library of Alexandria . . . paintings, architectural drawings, engineering schematics, medical studies. . . . It's incredible."

"Can we go inside and see?"

"No," Adrian responded quickly. "He's a little bit prickly . . . hard to deal with . . . even in heaven."

"What's his problem?"

"He's one of the few people everybody agrees is a genius. That's a lot to carry around for sixty-seven years on the earth and nearly five hundred years up here. He's always trying to live up to it. Sometimes it makes him a bit temperamental."

"Did you ask him about the code?"

"What?" Adrian looked puzzled.

"You know, the da Vinci code. Did he really paint all those clues in the *Last Supper*?"

Adrian grimaced and shushed Al firmly.

"Don't bring that up! He doesn't know anything about it. If he finds out about that book"—Adrian rolled his eyes—"heaven help us! You should have heard the stink he raised when he found out the Wright brothers had built a working airplane. He had drawn schematics for a flying machine four hundred years earlier and accused them of stealing his idea. Then he saw how Copernicus and Galileo were building telescopes and accused them of the same thing. Then he was fit to be tied when he saw twentieth-century chemists restoring parts of the *Mona Lisa* and the *Last Supper* paintings. He shouted they might as well paint excrement on the canvases! He wanted them flogged. He's caused such a stir up here that they gave him his re-created Florence home just to shut him up."

Suddenly, da Vinci swept back onto the portico, this time holding a canvas and an easel. A tray holding globs of different-color paints was cleverly locked on the side of the easel.

"I need you to draw me an animal, Master," Adrian said softly as da Vinci loosened the paint tray and gently took hold of the paintbrush with his left hand.

"What kind of animal?" he demanded.

Adrian pointed to the street below. "Does the master see that horse down in the street? I would wish you to paint that horse." Directly below was a dark brown mare tied to a hitching post.

"But the horse is facing the wrong way!" da Vinci complained. "I can see only her backside from here."

"I know, Master. Paint what you can see."

"It is the responsibility of the artist to paint what he can see and to do it the justice of its reality," da Vinci said as he began focusing his powers of concentration.

Adrian and Al waited quietly while the master stroked and brushed, occasionally glancing at the subject in the street below. Finally, da Vinci put the brush down and stooped close to the canvas, his nose no more than a few inches from it. Expertly using his fingers, he spread and manipulated thin streaks of the paint until, finally satisfied, he straightened up and, without a word or a glance, disappeared into his studio. Adrian walked around to behold the master's work. He broke out in a broad grin, beckoning Al to come around and see. Da Vinci had faithfully re-created the butt end of the horse, in large, bold strokes and accurate colors, omitting no detail of the anatomy. Rather than using the street background, da Vinci had used a series of thinning lines to make it look like the horse was standing in an open field.

"You had da Vinci paint a horse's ass?" Al asked incredulously.

Adrian laughed. "What's good enough for Mister Ed's proctologist is good enough for da Vinci."

℮〜 They were back in the sun-flooded conservatory, the new painting on the easel covered in the same cloth. Adrian leaned casually on the tea table, patiently waiting, while Al stood at the wall of glass, soaking in the outside scenery. It had never occurred to him that he would, or could, be rich, and he never thought he wanted to be. Just enough to get by comfortably had always been his credo. He admired the flower beds, the shrubberies, and the spurting fountain that decorated the grounds. The Tomlinsons probably spent more on outside decor than he spent buying his last house. For the first time, he began to wonder if he could have hit a big financial payday if he had put his mind to it. If it meant having to deal with people like Morgan Telford all the time, he was glad he never put his mind to it. He began to hear voices coming and turned to join Adrian at the table.

A few moments later, the Tomlinsons walked into the room with Morgan holding Mr. Tomlinson's arm. Merriman Tomlinson, white-haired, angular, and walking with a shuffle, was beaming at the attention being paid to him by this younger woman. Eliza Tomlinson, short, stooped, and dependent on a cane, followed slowly behind, her attitude seemingly resigned to the fact that her husband was going to enjoy visiting with this blonde. She stopped at the table and poured herself a cup of tea while Morgan escorted Mr. Tomlinson in front of the covered canvas.

"I hope you like my painting," she said, fluttering her eyelashes. "I may not be a great artist, but I have a great heart. And this painting"—she choked up slightly for effect, a tear welling in one eye—"whatever you think of it . . . is from my heart."

"I'm sure it is going to be lovely." Mr. Tomlinson patted her hand. Neither of them saw Eliza roll her eyes.

"Let's get on with it," Mrs. Tomlinson said impatiently. "I have a yoga class in half an hour!"

"I wanted to paint something that reminded me of you, Mrs. Tomlinson," Morgan continued, beaming momentarily at the old lady, then returning her admiring gaze to the woman's husband. "I spent a lot of time wondering how to best express her attributes on canvas and how I could best portray what I thought of her." Mrs. Tomlinson sipped her tea and cast a wary eye at Morgan.

"Let's just see what you did, honey," she said, walking in front of the painting. She tried to remove the cloth cover, but between the cup of tea and the cane, she was having difficulty.

"I'll do that!" Morgan jumped over, took a deep breath, and grabbed the cloth. "Here it is!" She pulled the cover up and away. Instead of looking at the painting, Morgan kept her eyes fixed on the old couple so she could gauge their reaction. Mrs. Tomlinson's eyes bugged out of her head, and Mr. Tomlinson's expression melted quickly from a smile to outright horror as he threw his gnarled, shaking hand up to his mouth. Morgan finally glanced at the painting, and after a quick double take, her bugging eyes gave Eliza's a run for the money.

"Young lady," Mr. Tomlinson said firmly, his body shaking from anger, "is this supposed to be a joke? It's not the least bit funny!"

"I suppose I should take it as a compliment," Mrs. Tomlinson said diffidently. "Most people have called me a bitch all my life. Being a horse's ass is a step up."

"There's been a mix-up." Morgan began stammering an explanation.

"Consider yourself fortunate I remember how a gentleman treats a lady, no matter the circumstance!" the old man blurted out in the strongest voice his aging throat could muster.

"This is a mistake. . . ." Morgan implored him.

"The mistake was meeting you!" Mrs. Tomlinson shouted. "Look how you have upset my husband!" The old lady whipped her teacup at the painting and it exploded in a rain of brown liquid. The cup bounced off the painting and it hit the floor, shattering into a thousand splinters. Morgan and the old man both jumped back, startled.

"My dear!" Mr. Tomlinson reached out for his wife to calm her. "This is still her painting! You've ruined it!"

"Oh, don't worry," the old woman replied, looking contemptuously at Morgan. "It's not like it was a da Vinci or something. We'll have Raymond give her the five bucks it's worth." She took her husband's elbow. Mr. Tomlinson gave Morgan one last befuddled look, then began walking with his wife, the two of them muttering and shuffling out of the room.

Morgan watched the rivulets of tea run down the painting. Between the anger and the embarrassment, she was shaking so hard, her head hurt. Where was that snide little driver Adrian? Somehow he was involved in this, she convinced herself. She stormed out the side door and around to the front of the mansion. Her limousine was gone.

The limo, minus its backseat passenger, weaved through New York City traffic again.

"I'd call that proper restitution," Adrian said. "Wouldn't you?"

"Yes." Al smiled, satisfied. "I guess she won't be leaving messages on anybody's answering machine for a while."

"Or going to Hollywood." Adrian swerved the car into an empty lot under an elevated highway. "You happy with the way things have turned out so far?"

"Except for the fact we stranded the gorgeous blonde on Long Island and you went skinny-dipping with the fat old bartender, I think everything is perfect."

"Who do we HARP on next?" he asked.

"That depends," Al replied. "Can I pick someone who was a bigger jerk to someone else than they were to me?" Adrian put the car in park and began drumming the steering wheel.

"I don't think anybody ever asked that before." He thought for a moment. "I guess it's all right as long as this jerk influenced your life, too. Who did you have in mind?"

"Harvey W. Baumgartner—a shyster posing as an investment broker. He convinced my parents to put their life savings in a special investment fund; turns out the fund was nothing more than his personal bank account. My parents might as well have invested in Three Mile Island or the Bay City Rollers or Enron."

"They lost everything?" Adrian asked.

"Yes."

"Sounds like Harvey is a good candidate." Adrian whipped out his HEAVEN box, but after a few moments, he shook his head. "Nope. You're out of luck this time, Al. Mr. Baumgartner is no longer on the earth. He died six years ago. He's up here with us now."

"How come he's not in . . . you know, in the other place?" Adrian pointed downward. "And I don't mean the civilization living on the bottom of your shoes."

"That's not for me to say," Adrian said seriously.

"So I don't get the chance to get some payback against this guy?"

"Not necessarily. You can flag him if you want."

"What does that mean?"

"Flagging is what we do to people who are already up here and then get accused of being a jerk. If you're flagged, your rights and privileges are suspended until you answer the charges before a special tribunal. If it turns out you were a jerk, you have to perform what you'd call community service and what we call penitence before all your rights and privileges are restored. If you want, I can flag ol' Harvey until your parents join us. Then he can answer for what he did."

"Flag him!" Al said without thinking about it. Adrian touched a small button on the HEAVEN box console. A large red flag appeared on the screen. He touched it and the flag disappeared, followed by a loud ping.

"Okay." Adrian smiled, satisfied. "Mr. Baumgartner has been flagged."

"If I can't get Harvey Baumgartner, then I'm going back to my college years again," Al said. "A guy by the name of Dalton James. Everybody knows him as Dean James."

"The baseball player and broadcaster?" Adrian looked surprised. "What kind of problem could you possibly have with him?" Before Al could answer, Adrian raised his hand. "Hold on a moment."

CHAPTER 13

the third jerk al mitchell
meets on earth

*T*HE MIST SWIRLED around them again, only this time it
lifted quickly thanks to a refreshing breeze Al could feel touch his
face. He was shocked at the scene of utter devastation that surrounded him. He and Adrian were standing in the middle of a
wreck that once was a baseball stadium. A two-tiered grandstand
circled the playing field, except in center and right fields, where an
ugly, crumbling wall of concrete and corrugated iron completed
the park. The upper grandstand was exhausted and sagging, especially behind home plate, where much of it had collapsed onto the
lower tier. The roof above it was a tortured relic. Most of the sheet
metal was gone, exposing ugly, twisted support beams and long

stretches of the sky above. There was the black-carbon signature of fire streaked along the facade and walls, and long-settled soot masked the once robust red of what chairs remained on both tiers.

"Boy, you take me to all the classy places," Al said, noticing trash strewn all about the field. He kicked a crushed beer can laying near his foot, and it flew a few feet before deflecting off the rusted remains of a pile of car motors, near where second base probably was, the pinging noise of the deflection echoing off the ghostly grandstand. "What do you call this architecture? Early American tornado?"

"Pitiful, isn't it?" Adrian said mournfully. "This place used to be very famous."

"For what? Artillery practice?"

"No, for baseball. This is Shibe Park," Adrian said. "Since your next jerk is a baseball player, I thought we'd start here . . . one of my favorite places."

"I heard of Shibe Park—Philadelphia, right?"

"Home of the Philadelphia Athletics for forty-five years"— Adrian nodded—"until the dark day they moved to Kansas City . . . and then Oakland."

"They sure let this place go to hell." Al looked for the familiar green-and-brown pattern of a baseball diamond, but the only brown he saw came from the rotting piles of trash and the putrid liquid seeping from the abandoned motors. The only green came from patches of weeds sprouting out of the dusty ground and through the cracks of the concrete.

"They closed the park in 1970 and used it as a junkyard until they tore it down six years later," Adrian said. "Breaks my heart to see it this way."

"Then why did you take us here?"

"Because I love to do this. . . ." Adrian had a sudden glee in his voice. Almost immediately, the park began to renovate itself. The grandstand became young, upright, and elegant in a fresh coat of paint—the facade a relaxing blue, the seats a vibrant red. The outfield wall reassembled itself. The rusted motors disassembled into smaller and smaller parts, spreading across the ground until the parts became the rich brown dirt of the infield. The trash and the weeds shriveled and spread out on the ground until transformed into a manicured lawn.

"That's more like it!" Adrian beamed, walking toward the seats behind home plate with Al following. "This is the way it looked the first time I came here as a boy in 1928. What a great team they had."

"Sorry if I disagree, but I'm a Yankee fan."

"Yeah?" Adrian challenged him. "The '28 team had more Hall of Famers than any other team in history . . . Foxx, Cochrane, Simmons, Collins, Grove, Speaker, Cobb, Connie Mack. The Yankees can't say that. And from '29 to '31, they were the best team in baseball. They wiped out everybody, including the mighty Yankees." Adrian turned more subdued. "But nobody ever calls them the best team of all time because nobody remembers that Philadelphia even had the Athletics." Adrian climbed over the low wall into the grandstand and sat down.

"I didn't realize you liked baseball so much," Al said, following him over the wall.

"When I was a kid, I did. As I got older, I found sports more exciting when the outcome of the game directly improved my financial situation, if you know what I mean."

"You mean you were betting on the games?"

"No, I was conducting 'Hallelujah Chorus' for the Mormon Tabernacle Choir every time the A's hit a home run. Of course, I mean betting. I spent more time under the first base grandstand than I did in my seat. We would get odds on who was going to win, who was going to score the first run, who was going to get the first hit, or who was going to fall down drunk in the dugout. The A's were known to do that now and then." He pulled out the HEAVEN box. As Al sat down, a sudden sharp crack could be heard—the unmistakable sound of a baseball being hit solidly by a wooden bat. It was immediately followed by a huge roar from a phantom crowd. As the roar died down, a voice came over the stadium's public address system.

"Ladies and gentlemen, now coming up . . . Dalton James." With that, a holographic image appeared from the first base dugout.

Al snickered at the image. "That's him."

James's image floated toward home plate—college-age youthful, he was surprisingly thin and narrow-shouldered, his posture flawlessly erect. Yellow hair flowed from the sides and back of his scuffed batting helmet, but his attempt at a beard was limited to a few light curly locks around his chin. He was wearing a tight double-knit baseball uniform of white with dark blue trim, with the scripted lettering "Cal State" across his chest. He took his stance in the batter's box and stared out at the pitcher's mound.

"Dalton James was born and raised in southern California," the PA announcer continued, "where he set a record for the highest batting average and the lowest SATs at his high school in the same year. He was an all-American wide receiver his freshman year in college, where he wore number 88—some say in tribute to his IQ.

These same people say he turned his attention from football to baseball because the scores were lower and easier to count, but it was really because scouts told him he had a good chance to sign with a pro team. He eventually made it to the major leagues, where he was a lifetime .292 hitter over ten years, before a shoulder injury ended his career abruptly. For the past nine years, he has been a featured announcer on the *Game of the Week*. He is a very popular TV personality if not a very popular person."

"He's not such a nice guy, I hear," Adrian said.

"He's only nice to baseball players and people who can help him. He's been like that since I first knew him."

"What's your beef with him?"

"We played college ball together," Al replied. "He was our center fielder and the big star. He was a real prima donna, always worried about himself, never the team. The year I was a junior, Dean was a senior, and he had major-league scouts all over him. We had this new player transfer from Arizona . . . Alberto Gonzalez. He was a very good player and scouts were beginning to take some notice, which ol' Deanie couldn't deal with. . . ."

June 1980

> *Al raised his arm to block the sunlight with his baseball glove, tracking the flight of the batted baseball through the holes in the webbing. He took a few steps backward and the ball nestled in the pocket of his glove. One of the things Al loved most about playing was the special feeling of baseball's pregame rituals . . . putting on the uniform, taking batting practice, and*

*especially standing in the outfield with teammates,
soaking in the sun on the fresh-cut grass, shagging fly
balls, and talking about everything from the game to
girls. It was the baseball players' version of sitting
under the hair dryer at the beauty parlor and gossiping.
Standing shoulder to shoulder with Al in the outfield
was his best friend on the team, third baseman Rico
Pantelli.*

*"Deanie Weanie struck last night," Rico said. "He
talked Coach Critten into taking Gonzo off the team."*

*"I can't believe that!" Al said, more angry than
shocked. "Why would Coach do it?"*

*"Deanie's father is one of Coach's best friends, not
to mention a big alumni contributor. They're both out to
make sure Deanie gets signed by a major-league scout.
Gonzo was diverting attention from Deanie, so he had
to go."*

*"Who the hell is running this team?" Al whipped
the ball back to the infield angrily.*

*"Critten has his nose so far up Deanie's ass,
Deanie's got two Adam's apples."*

*Al stewed for a few moments as he watched the
flight of another batted ball soar over his head. Instead
of chasing the ball, Al started jogging in toward the
infield.*

*"I think you misjudged it." Rico pointed to the ball
landing far behind Al. "Where you going?"*

*"To talk to Dean." Al waved Rico to join him and
the pair jogged through the infield, into the third base*

dugout, and up the tunnel runway into the cramped locker room. A few players were still lingering, getting dressed, doing stretching exercises. Dean was sitting on the bench in front of his locker, concentrating on the newspaper folded in his lap. The paper was opened to the crossword puzzle. Dean was drumming the paper with a pencil.

"He does crossword puzzles?" Al whispered disbelievingly to Rico.

"His English professor told him it would help him build his vocabulary," Rico replied.

"He doesn't think Deanie can get by on the ten words he already knows?"

Dean looked up and greeted his teammates. "Hey, guys! Seven-letter word for "hottest place on earth."

"Easy. Rico's bedroom," Panelli said.

"Funny," Dean replied dryly. "I'm sure that's true for all the Boy Scouts in the neighborhood." Dean looked to Al. "Come on, Al Tuna Man! Help me out." He held up the puzzle. It was completely blank.

"You're still working on the first clue?" Rico laughed.

"It's a pretty tough puzzle," Dean said defensively, pulling the newspaper back. "You got to start somewhere. The clue for one across is 'hottest place on earth'. . . seven letters."

Al shrugged. "What do you think it is?"

"I think it's Africa," Dean said proudly, flattered that Al actually asked his opinion. Dean began filling in the boxes, spelling it as he went. "A-F-F-R-I-C-A."

"Deano," Al said. "There's only one F in Africa."

Dean looked down at the puzzle, his face wrinkled.

"But then it doesn't fit!" he shouted with childlike frustration, then quickly calmed down. "Are there two C's?"

"I think the word you want is equator.*" Al winked.*

"You guys pulling my chain again?" Dean looked suspiciously at Al. "I never heard of that country." He looked down at the paper again. "E-K-W-A-T-E-R," he spelled out loud, and then looked up, smiling. "It fits!"

Just then, Coach Critten stuck his head in the locker room "Everybody get your ass on the field now!" Dean jumped up and tossed the newspaper in his locker and grabbed his glove. "Got to make a pit stop first," he said, veering into the connecting bathroom.

"E-K-W-A-T-E-R?" Rico asked. "It's a good thing breathing is a reflex, or we'd be out a center fielder."

"I'd say he was dumb as a brick, but I don't want to insult the bricks." Al wiped the sweat from his forehead as Dean emerged.

"You guys still here? You better get outside before Coach gets pissed."

"I just wanted to ask you about Gonzo," Al said.

Dean gave Al a look of distaste. "He told Coach last night he wouldn't be able to play the rest of the season."

"He didn't say that," Rico said angrily. "I was there. He said he couldn't play until he found someone to look after his sick mom."

Dean shrugged nonchalantly. "He said he can't find

anybody to take care of her, so he was going to do it himself."

"Yeah, only after Coach told Gonzo he wouldn't play him anymore."

"Why?" Al asked Rico.

"Because Coach said Gonzo would be worried about his mom and not concentrate on the games."

"That's a crock." Al turned back to Dean.

"Hey!" Dean snapped, looking at Rico darkly. "Why are you guys busting my balls? I don't know what Gonzalez said! Maybe if Gonzalez knew how to talk good English, we'd all understand what he was talking about better. Besides, who are you guys trying to fool? You don't want taco breath on the team any more than I do." Dean headed out of the locker room.

Rico turned to Al. "Two across . . . the clue is Dean James."

"J-E-R-K." Al replied.

"We came close to winning the national championship that year." Al sighed. "If we'd had Gonzo all year, I bet we would have won it all. Deano didn't care. He got signed, got his bonus, and wound up in the major leagues."

"James turned out to be a pretty good big-league ballplayer." Adrian winked. "I won a little on him now and then."

"At least Gonzo made it to the majors, too," Al said. "He played a few years and now he's a manager. I keep hearing his name come up as a candidate to manage the U.S. team in the new World Baseball Tournament."

"Yeah." Adrian grinned mischievously. "Do you know who is campaigning for that position against Gonzalez? None other than Dean James!"

℮᷉ Dean James stood next to the Dairy Association of America mascot and did not look happy. A decade past his retirement from the game, he looked considerably older. His light, closely cropped hair did not betray much gray, but his widow's peak had climbed to the crown of his head. His love of beer and fine food had long ago overwhelmed his desire to stay in any kind of shape. He was very self-conscious about his massive gut and always wore loose, California surfer clothes even though he knew he wasn't fooling anyone. Being so overweight made him particularly uncomfortable standing under the relentlessly hot and blindingly bright battery of studio lights. Most annoying was the young actor named Evan who was playing the dairy association mascot. Evan was too small for the cow costume he was wearing, and he was having a difficult time with the heavy plastic cow head. Every time Evan moved, the head tilted over and whacked Dean on the top of his head.

The director, a wiry, hypertensive man in a safari jacket and wide-brimmed hat, was pacing in front of the nerve-frayed production crew.

"Are we ready?" he snapped to the cameraman.

"As soon as the cow is." The cameraman shrugged.

"Anytime you are ready, Evan," the director called out in a very snippy voice.

"Okay," the actor called out. "Don't be such a grouch!"

"Who's a grouch?" the director feigned innocence. "You know the way I work, Evan. Whenever I film a milk commercial, I like to do forty-three takes just to get a shot of someone drinking the milk."

"I'm trying as best I can," Evan said apologetically, "This is one heavy cow's head."

"Perhaps we will grind it up and do a commercial for the beef association afterward," the director replied.

"Good idea, assuming you let me out of the costume first."

"I make no such promises," the director said as he pointed to a young girl standing near him and she quickly darted onto the set, handing Dean a tall glass of milk. Dean winced.

"If I have to drink another glass of warm milk, I'm going to turn into a walking piece of cheese," he groaned.

"All right," the director said, ignoring him, "remember when you hug each other to hold the hug until I yell, 'Cut!'"

"Hey!" Dean shouted. "If you cut me, you'll be cutting the cheese!" He began laughing loudly, drowning out the smattering of guffaws in the room. The director looked around, puzzled.

"This is funny? Why is this funny?" he said impatiently. The crew went silent. On the call of "Ready!" Dean forced a broad grin on his face, and on the call of "Action" he enthusiastically gulped down the milk, much to the animated delight of the mascot. When Dean held up the empty glass, the cow joyously wrapped its arms around Dean. They held the happy pose a few seconds until the director called, "Cut!" at which point Dean's smile vanished and he pushed the mascot away. There was a smattering of applause as the director said, "Print."

Adrian watched from the fringes of the studio. He could see his reflection in the glass of the production booth and he spent a moment straightening his yellow silk tie. Blue suit, wing tips . . .

Adrian looked quite the executive. From the swarm around Dean James came a man in an equally spiffy business suit who rushed over to Adrian, hand extended.

"Are you Mr. Adrian? Nice to meet you. I'm C. Laurence Quinlan, Mr. James's business manager and attorney."

"Hi." Adrian shook his hand. "What should I call you? Laurence? Larry? C?"

"Larry will do quite fine." Quinlan laughed and took Adrian by the elbow until they were within a few feet of Dean, who was signing autographs for the mostly female members of the production crew.

"Don't forget this Sunday night . . . *Game of the Week* . . . Yankees against the Orioles," Dean said as he accepted each piece of paper and signed. Quinlan approached and whispered something into Dean's ear as he finished the last of the autographs. Not looking very pleased, Dean nudged Quinlan away from the disbursing crowd.

"What the hell are you doing?" Dean seethed under his breath. "I got an important interview with National Sports Radio in an hour and instead of getting ready, I'm sitting here getting hugged by numb-nuts in an oversized cow suit . . . and now I have to talk to who?"

"He's an executive with the dairy association and just wanted to meet you."

Dean's face clenched.

"Larry . . . what the hell are you doing? Nobody can be this incompetent by accident. You know how much I want to be coach of the U.S. World Baseball Team, don't you?"

"Yes," Quinlan answered.

"And you know how much this interview with National Sports Radio in an hour means to me, don't you?"

"Yes, Dean."

"And you know how much I hate having to glad-hand every schmuck who wants to meet a famous baseball player, don't you?" Quinlan nodded silently.

"Okay. Then explain to me why the hell you are making me meet someone I don't want to meet and not helping me get ready to do what I need to do. Sounds like I should fire your ass right now!"

"It'll only be a minute," Quinlan pleaded. "You have to say hi and be nice. It's in your contract with the dairy association. Remember? You took the extra five thousand for the provision that if any of their members showed up wherever you were, you would take the time to say hello."

"Make it quick," Dean growled as Quinlan waved Adrian over.

"Meet Dean James," Quinlan said.

"Wow! How exciting!" Adrian played it to the hilt. "I'm a big fan, Mr. James. I watch you all the time on the *Game of the Week.*"

"Thanks for those very nice words," Dean said robotically. "What's your name?"

"Adrian." They shook hands.

"What do you do for the dairy association?"

Adrian hadn't expected that question. He wasn't ready for it.

"I'm . . . uh . . . vice president of . . . cow procurement for the eastern region."

"Cow procurement!" Dean nodded with a plastic smile, then shot a get-me-out-of-here glance at his agent. "Sounds beyond great," he said with only a modicum of enthusiasm. Dean took Adrian's hand and shook it vigorously. "Nice to talk to you."

"I hope you're having a good time with us today, Mr. James," Adrian continued, not letting go of Dean's hand. "Milk is so important to the health and well-being of our kids."

"That's what I heard," Dean replied. "I drink it a lot and I never cry when it's spilt." Adrian forced a side-splitting laugh.

"Oh, that's really good, Mr. James." He stopped laughing. "I was wondering if you would consider making a second commercial for us."

"I don't think so," Dean snapped.

"It would be for the Spanish-speaking fans."

Dean thought a moment.

"Sorry. I don't think I should do it. I don't speak a word of Spanish. You should get someone who speaks Spanish." Dean giggled. "Get Al Gonzalez to do it." Dean gave his manager a sly grin. "Then he'd be too busy to coach the U.S. World Baseball Team." As Dean and Quinlan both laughed, the director made his way over.

"I'd like to get a couple more shots," he said hesitantly, "maybe Mr. James in a baseball uniform."

"No. I won't put on a uniform anymore. I'm too fat these days." Dean patted his protruding gut. "No thanks."

"Well, then how about one more shot of you with the cow?"

"No, thanks," Dean snapped. "I don't want anything to do with that cow."

"Mr. James is kind of tired," Quinlan explained to the director.

"You bet I'm tired. I've been going full tilt for a long time and I need some rest," Dean pleaded.

The director mulled it over a few minutes. "I suppose we should call it a wrap."

"Can't come soon enough for me," Dean said.

"All right, it's a wrap." The director turned to Dean. "We're having a little wrap-up party in the next room if you care to join us."

"Not me," Dean blurted out. "I'm done." Quinlan sighed as he watched the insulted director walk away.

"Dean, you want me to take you back to the hotel?" Quinlan asked.

"Yes! Yes! Absolutely yes!" replied an exasperated Dean, who walked past Adrian without another word.

Al accompanied Adrian into the posh King William Hotel. They stopped just inside the doorway and watched Dean James enter the dimly lit cocktail bar just off the lobby. Adrian pulled a small vial out of his pocket and looked at his watch. "Dean's interview is in twenty minutes. We have to act fast. Here's what we do. We go in the bar and I introduce you. Since you used to play ball with him, he'll probably be happy to see you, since he's usually nice to fellow ballplayers." Adrian held up the vial. "You talk to him while I get a couple of drops of this into his drink."

"What is it?"

"It'll put him out like a light. It's slow acting, so once he drinks it, we have a few minutes to get him out of the bar and up to his room."

"Then what?"

"Worry about the rest later," Adrian said.

The two men crossed the lobby and entered the bar. Other than a few people sitting at the cocktail tables and Dean James standing at an end of the bar accepting a bottle of water from the bartender, the place was empty. As the men slowly approached, Dean watched them warily. He recognized Adrian, but his reaction did not suggest a warm welcome.

"Dairy association guy, right?" Dean asked.

"That's me!" Adrian grinned. "VP of cow procurement. I wanted to thank you again for today—"

"Fine." A disinterested Dean turned away, but Adrian continued.

"And I want to introduce you to my associate, whom I think you know from your college days. This is Al Mitchell." Suddenly Dean turned and brightened.

"Al Mitchell! Oh, yeah!" said Dean with a flicker of recognition. "Shortstop from Birmingham! We called you Al-a-bama, right?"

"No. You got your Als mixed up. I was the guy from New Jersey. I'm the one who ate tuna fish all the time." Dean pondered for a moment and then brightened again.

"Al Tuna!" Dean shouted triumphantly, and broke into a bigger laugh.

"That's me!" Al replied just as loudly.

"Sure, I remember you! The tuna fish eater! You smelled like a fishing pier at low tide!"

The two embraced with a laugh, and in the midst of their bear hug, Adrian deftly waved his hand over Dean's water bottle. Al only caught the tail end of Adrian's motion, but he saw the drops from his small vial cause a ripple in the water bottle. Having noticed none of it, Dean kept pounding Al on the back.

"So! Al Tuna! Your friend here is vice president of cow procurement. What are you? Vice president of milking?" Dean picked up his water bottle but began laughing again. He set the bottle back on the bar without drinking. "Al Tuna!" he repeated to Adrian. "Isn't that a great name?" Adrian forced a smile and looked at his watch. It was quarter to three. . . . Time was getting short.

"He's got to drink that water before he goes upstairs," he whispered in Al's ear. Al nodded that he understood.

"Can we buy you a drink?" Al asked.

"Not now, thanks. I've got an important interview in a few minutes and I want to be on top of my game."

"What's the interview about?" Al asked.

"I'm going to tell the world why I should be the coach of the U.S. World Baseball Team and not Gonzo Gonzalez! You remember Gonzo Gonzalez, don't you?" Dean asked Al.

"Yeah . . . I remember Gonzo. He was on the team my junior year—"

"Until I sent him packing back to Arizona, where he belonged." Dean finished the sentence, then his mood turned darker. "I'm going to send him packing again."

"What do you mean?" Al asked.

"I'm going to tell the world that Gonzo Gonzalez is not fit to be coach of the U.S. team. He's been running around with another woman . . . a young girl . . . and the last thing the U.S. World Baseball Team needs is a coach who has a paternity suit slapped on him by an eighteen-year-old girl."

"Wow!" Adrian said. "Is this true?"

Dean smiled wryly. "It will be by the time I'm done with the interview."

Adrian nudged Al, indicating the bottle of water again. Oblivious to this, Dean kept talking, pointing to a pair of men sitting at one of the cocktail tables. "You see those two guys? They're from one of the top sports equipment manufacturers in the world. When I'm named coach, I'm going to see that they get exclusive merchandising rights for the U.S. World Baseball Team. And to demonstrate their gratitude, they're giving me ten percent right off the top. I'll make more from this deal than everything else in my life put together!" He looked at his watch. "In fact, I should go." He grabbed Al by his arms. "Good to see you, Al Tuna! Listen, I'm in 628. If you're around later, come by and we'll break open a real bottle."

"Thanks. Don't forget your water," Al said, handing the bottle to Dean.

"Nah, thanks," Dean refused the bottle. "I can't drink it. I drank so much milk this afternoon, I feel like going outside and chewing on the grass for a while." He nodded at Adrian and headed out of the bar.

"You were supposed to get him to drink the water," a frustrated Adrian said.

"What did you want me to do? Put two straws in the bottle like we were on a date and have him sip it with me? Maybe I should have wrestled him to the ground and poured it down his throat . . . or just pleaded with him to drink it because we wanted him to pass out. The question is, what do we do now?"

"Get up to Room 628!" Adrian said.

℃ Adrian and Al stepped off the elevator and hurried down the sixth floor, stopping in front of Room 628. Adrian looked at his watch. Eight minutes to three. He took an old-fashioned atomizer perfume bottle from his pocket. The bottle was only about an inch in height and the round atomizer attached to it was a gaudy pink color with purple flourishes.

"What is that?" Al demanded. "Perfume?"

"Same stuff as in the vial. Only it works a lot faster. This will knock him out in a couple of seconds."

"What is it. Eau de Mike Tyson?"

Adrian ignored the comment and rapped on the door. No answer. He rapped a second time.

"Not now, I'm busy," Dean's surly voice finally responded.

"Urgent message from Mr. Quinlan," Adrian called out. "He said you should read it before your three o'clock interview." After a few moments and some audible griping, Dean opened the door. He immediately recognized the pair.

"Not now, Al! Look! I was nice to you guys downstairs. But that's enough!" Dean began to shut the door, but Adrian quickly fixed his leg in position to block it, swung the perfume bottle in front of Dean's face, and began squeezing the atomizer bulb. The former ballplayer stood startled as waves of spray whipped into his jowly face.

"Are you done?" he asked Adrian, wiping away the mist on his cheeks. Adrian nodded. "I guess it's too much to hope that that was either Viagra or a weight-loss spray." Dean looked at Al again. "I think your friend needs help. Now, if you don't mind, I have important things to do!" Dean put both hands on the door as if he were about to forcibly slam it. He suddenly gasped for breath, snapped upright, gave Al a quizzical look, and pitched forward without another sound, except for the loud groan Al let out at the weight he was suddenly supporting.

"Get him inside," Adrian urged, pushing the door all the way open, then grabbing Dean's shoulders.

"Jeez! He's huge!" Al grunted as they dragged James' dead weight toward the bed. "This guy's got his own gravitational pull." They heaved Dean onto the bed. "Deano!" Al let out a breath of relief. "I've got two words that will change your life forever—*salad bar*!"

Dean let slip a muffled moan. Al climbed onto the mattress and pinched Dean's cheek and tried to pry open one of his eyes. "Is he all right?"

"Leave him alone," Adrian said. "He's out of it!"

"He's not out! He's safe!" Dean slurred energetically, lifting his head slightly off the pillow. "He slid around the tag! Pitch him low and inside, so he can't extend his arms!" Dean began to lose consciousness. "Take it . . . one game . . . at . . . a time." He barely got the last word out of his mouth before his head dropped on the pillow. Adrian checked his watch again. It was just about three o'clock.

"What do you do now? Imitate Dean's voice in the interview?"

"No," Adrian replied, as if offended. "That would be crass and dishonest. It would be against the code of HARP." Adrian smiled benignly. "Dean is going to do the interview himself." Adrian pulled out his HEAVEN box and opened it.

Dean's voice played back through the box's speaker. "Sounds beyond great . . . nice to talk to you . . . I'm too fat these days."

"I recorded everything he said earlier today."

Just then, the telephone in Dean's room rang, and Adrian's smile turned up a few watts. He picked up the phone. "Hello. This is Mr. James's room."

"Hi, this is the producer of the *Craig Clyburn Show* for National Sports Radio. We're going on-air in one minute with a live interview with Mr. James and Craig."

"Right," Adrian replied. "Dean is right here. I'll put him on." Adrian deftly attached the HEAVEN box to the telephone receiver.

"Mr. James?" the producer asked.

"Hi. Nice to talk to you." Dean's recorded voice played over the phone.

"Hi, Mr. James. I just want you to know what a big fan I am of yours."

"Thanks for those very nice words," Dean's voice responded back.

"Craig will be coming live to you in a minute."

"Sounds beyond great!"

"Okay, stand by," the producer said. They heard a click and could hear the radio broadcast faintly through the receiver.

"Did you really eat that much tuna fish?" Adrian asked Al.

"Cats in the neighborhood treated me as one of their own," Al explained.

Suddenly Craig Clyburn's voice was audible through the HEAVEN box.

"Welcome back to the *Craig Clyburn Show* on National Sports Radio. Time now to talk to one of America's best-known baseball voices. Dean James joins us from his hotel room in New York. Dean, are you there?"

"Nice to talk to you," came back Dean's recorded voice.

"Dean, how are you doing?"

"I'm too fat these days."

Clyburn laughed. "I guess we all have that problem, Dean. How's your wife?"

"I don't want anything to do with that cow."

"Uh . . . well," Clyburn began stuttering nervously, "I hope Mrs. James is not in listening range . . . unless that's a term of endearment you guys have."

"Who cares?" Dean's voice responded.

"Maybe we should get right to the topic at hand." Clyburn sounded worried.

"Can't come quick enough for me."

"I can see that." Clyburn cleared his throat. "In the next couple of days, baseball is going to decide on its world tournament coach. Apparently it's down to two people . . . you and Al Gonzalez."

"That's what I heard."

"You want the job?" Clyburn asked.

"I don't think I should do it—"

"You don't?" Clyburn cut in, sounding surprised. "Everybody says you are actively campaigning for the job."

"I won't put on a uniform anymore."

"You don't want to be coach of the U.S. World Baseball Team?"

"No, thanks. I'm tired. I've been going full tilt for a long time and I need some rest."

"Then who should do the coaching job?" Clyburn asked again.

"Get Al Gonzalez to do it."

"You are officially pulling yourself out of consideration?"

"Sounds beyond great!"

"And you're endorsing Al Gonzalez as the next coach of the U.S. World Baseball Team?"

"Yes! Yes! Absolutely yes!"

"Okay, Dean. Thanks very much for your time. There you have it, ladies and gentlemen, National Sports Radio breaks another exclusive! Dean James pulls out of consideration to be coach of the U.S. World Baseball Team!"

Adrian detached the HEAVEN box and hung up the phone.

"That takes care of that."

℘ The shrill ring of the telephone in Dean James's quiet hotel room snapped him out of his sleep. Still a bit groggy, and not realizing how long he had been sleeping, Dean groped for the phone and picked it up.

"Yes?" he rasped into the receiver. "This is Dean James." He sat up quickly. "Oh . . . I thought you were National Sports Radio. . . . You have my wife on the line? What does she want? . . . She's mad? What could she possibly be mad about?"

CHAPTER 14

the fourth jerk al mitchell meets on earth

*T*HE WHITE MIST transported Al and Adrian to the soft-backed seats of a railroad car that Al estimated was of an early-twentieth-century vintage. The walls boasted a shiny oak veneer; the floor, buffed and shined, gave no trace of a shoe or scuff mark. The train wasn't moving particularly fast—maybe thirty or thirty-five miles an hour, passing through a wonderfully green valley of open fields and farms visible through the windows on both sides of the train. The only open window was the one directly next to Adrian, and through it they could hear the chugging of the engine motor, which provided a rhythm for the back-and-forth rocking of their car. The seats directly facing Al and Adrian were unoccupied—in fact, the entire passenger car was empty.

"Boy, I would have given anything to hear that phone call from Mrs. James!" Al put his feet up on the empty seat across from him. "Not too many people get to call their wives a cow on national radio and live to tell about it." Al chuckled, admiring the passing scenery. "Where are we headed now?"

Before Adrian could answer, a gentle voice tinged with a southern drawl called out from behind Al.

"Would you mind removing your feet from the seat in deference to our other passengers?"

"What other passengers?" Al looked up and over his head. The man standing in the aisle looked familiar—soft face like Adrian, closely cropped white hair, and a slow, deliberate manner.

"Hello, Magnolia." Adrian smiled. The name brought it back for Al. He had met Magnolia at the Five People You Meet in Heaven Complaint Desk. Only now Magnolia was wearing the classic black uniform and hat of a train conductor. Al sat up so Magnolia could sit down.

"Hello, Adrian." Magnolia sat stiff-backed and respectfully, extending his hand to Al. "I don't know if you remember me . . . Cameron T. Magnolia."

"I remember you." Al shook his hand. "Nice to see you again."

"I thought we might take a little train ride and get some help from Magnolia," Adrian explained. "He was a conductor in his lifetime."

"Yes, sir," Magnolia drawled proudly. "I ran the rails from Bangor, Maine, to New Orleans, Louisiana, for twenty-two years and then I did the Chicago to Los Angeles run for fifteen years."

"Al here is about to name his fourth jerk," Adrian said, turning to Al. "Who is it?"

Al's lips pursed and his face tightened. "His name is John G. Erie."

"And why do you have a grudge against John G. Erie?" Magnolia asked pleasantly.

"I spent a lot of years building my career at LoonaTechnologies." Al began unconsciously tapping his foot. "I worked my way up to a pretty good executive position in the company's marketing side. Then the company brought in John G. Erie as the new chief marketing officer."

"And he fired you, right?" Adrian said.

"Why?" Magnolia asked.

"Because he could," Al replied.

Magnolia reached out and put his hand on Al's vibrating leg. "You take it easy, young man. We'll take care of everything." Magnolia stood up and began walking up and down the aisle shouting in his best conductor's voice, "John G. Erie! Next stop John G. Erie!" As Magnolia sat down, this time across from Adrian, an image entered the car—the holograph of a short, thin man with a ducklike walk, hunched shoulders, and a permanent half-smile etched on his taut face. The image sat down in the seat opposite Al.

"Jerk!" Al growled. Magnolia put his hand on Al's still-vibrating leg.

"You calm down," he said sweetly.

"I can't help it when I think of what this guy did . . . not just to me but a lot of other good people. He lied to me and to a lot of other people. He was always so damn nervous . . . constantly looking around over his shoulder like a Mafia stool pigeon waiting for the bullet he knows is coming. I think he was afraid that any minute somebody was going to burst in the room and tell everyone what a fraud he was."

"It's all right." Magnolia spoke just above a whisper. "Mr. Erie here is a difficult man, I grant you that. But understand about this man that his ambition far outweighed his ability. At some level, in his mind, he knew this was the case and it dictated his manner and his demeanor."

July 2004

Monday morning meetings were murder, but this one was going to be particularly tough. This was to be one of those "strategy sessions" that the new chief marketing officer liked to call from time to time. The only problem, as Al saw it, was that no one in the meeting discussed strategy.

Al came into the conference room. Dick Lynn was the only person in the room and he was studying some bar graphs. Neither man looked very happy.

"Have you seen the latest results from the employee morale survey?" Dick asked. "They're the lowest scores ever. If I had to sum it up, I'd say the employees consider Mr. Erie abrasive, condescending, egotistical, and incompetent."

"I find that hard to believe," Al said. "I don't think he's that condescending."

"Listen to this." Dick began reading from one of the comments in the survey. "I want to change jobs and work for a nicer boss. Who would I consider a nicer boss? We could start with Attila the Hun. If the Huns don't have any openings, I'll consider Stalin or Jack the Ripper."

"Speaking of the Huns, the barbarians are at the gates." Al motioned to the door. John G. Erie was entering with a staff of ten minions, including Hope Himmelmann and Sam "Call Me Samuel" Venable, all of whom dutifully took seats around the conference table. It was not lost on Dick or Al that no one was sitting near them.

"Good morning," Erie said passionlessly. His minions replied enthusiastically, each seemingly wanting to out-good-morning everyone else. "We need to move quickly on an important project," Erie continued. "Sales are flat, so I want us to spend a little time rethinking how we market and sell communications to the public. To do that, I want us to understand how communications happens at its very core." Murmurs of approval bounced through the room. Dick caught Al's attention and surreptitiously rolled his eyes.

"Is everyone familiar with the famous evolutionary scale drawings that show the ape evolving into primitive man and finally into modern man? I want to do the same thing for communications," Erie said.

"John," Dick cut in. "I think our sales are flat because our two biggest competitors offered summer specials. Their lower prices are cutting into our market share because we didn't match them."

"Dick," John G. Erie said pompously. "I don't want to jump to conclusions like that. I want us to truly think this thing through and make sure the analysis and the solutions we come up with are valid and tackle the real

*problems we identify." Murmurs of approval in the room
echoed more loudly. "For instance, Dick, did you know
that plants, vines, and most growing things communicate
with one another? How does that happen?"*

"Not by telephone," Dick said. "I know that much."

*John G. Erie stared coldly at Dick for a moment,
then let loose a guffaw, which loosened a chorus of
laughs from his minions. "What I mean, Dick," he continued patiently, "is think about a pack of wolves. The
wolves can communicate within the pack as to who eats
first and who has to wait. How does that happen?"*

"I don't know." Dick sighed.

*"How about under the sea? Most species of sea life
communicate. How do they do it? For instance, how do
mollusks communicate? I want you to explore these
questions and whichever others you think pertinent and
come back to me with a project recommendation by
the end of the week." He turned to Hope. "You're in
charge," Erie said as he stood up. "Thank you. I have
another meeting to get to."*

*"One more thing very quickly before you go." Dick
raised the bar graphs into the air. "Have you seen the
latest employee morale scores? They are very low."*

*"Doesn't concern me." Erie waved off Dick dismis-
sively. "That's looking backward, into the past. I'm all
about looking forward, looking to the future only." With
that, his minions burst into applause.*

*"These are current surveys, John," Dick said over
the clapping, "and I think there are some issues here. . . ."*

"Were the surveys taken today?" Erie asked.

"No"—Dick struggled to maintain his professionalism—"over the previous few weeks."

"Then I would say they are in the past." Erie smiled smugly as his minions nodded in awe of his logic.

"Besides," interjected Hope, "if people are unhappy, they can leave. No one is stopping them."

"That's right." Erie nodded approvingly at Hope. "I suspect that if we fix our communications marketing strategies, and increase sales, we will fix the morale problem."

"Can I just clarify one thing?" Al asked.

"What?" Erie answered, growing impatient.

"You said you want us to trace the history of communications like on the evolutionary chart?"

"Yes."

"Isn't that looking into the past?"

Al's question brought Erie to an annoyed standstill and elicited an angry response. "You are looking at the history of communications only in the context of solving a current problem, not dwelling on the past for the sake of reminiscing about the good old days. If I have to explain the difference to you, then maybe you don't belong working here." With that, Erie left the room.

Al looked at Dick Lynn. "We can't look into the reasons why our employees are unhappy, but we can spend time figuring out how mollusks communicate!"

"Like John G. Erie said, all undersea creatures communicate," Venable lectured Al.

"Wonderful." Al smirked. "How many of them buy our phones?"

"Don't you understand that John G. Erie is trying to get us to think differently?" Hope stood up. "If you don't want to participate in this exercise, fine. But we are going to do it and we are going to take it seriously. I think we should start by identifying undersea species of life that can communicate."

"How about SpongeBob SquarePants?" Al replied. There were a few light snickers, but hardly anyone in the room wanted to be caught making light of a John G. Erie idea.

"Besides"—Al started to get worked up, ignoring the signals he was getting from Dick to shut up—"what in hell could happen to an average mollusk on an average day that he would need to communicate to the rest of the mollusk world?" Al cupped his hands over his mouth. "Hey! Guys! Just got back from a week's vacation at the Mariana Trench! It was real deep! You hear about poor Sammy? Got caught up in a fishing net last week. Now he's on a Red Lobster commercial."

"You should have seen how appalled those people were in the meeting room." Al laughed. "You would have thought I painted a mustache on the *Mona Lisa*."

"Don't say that." Adrian cringed. "That's the last thing da Vinci needs to hear."

"For the next few months, I was involved in less and less work. I talked to John G. Erie and he assured me that everything would be fine. Shortly after that, he forced Dick to fire a bunch of people, including me. He didn't have the guts to do it himself. He had Dick do his dirty work. And a month later, he fired Dick."

"There's no sense holding a grudge or hating the man," Magnolia said in his slow drawl. "Don't do you no good in the end. Most everybody gets fired at least once in their life."

"I know, Magnolia. My problem isn't with what he did as much as it is with the way he did it. Do you know how he fired Dick? He left Dick a message on his answering machine at home on a Sunday night. Said Dick didn't have to bother coming in Monday, except to clean out his desk."

"Maybe we should hook him up with Morgan Telford," Adrian deadpanned.

"Is there any way you can target John G. Erie but help Dick Lynn as well?" Al asked. "I know he was getting desperate financially."

"Dick is in line for a job at a company called Eastern Wireless Communications," Adrian said.

"I know. He told me the night I . . . fell off the merry-go-round. Can you help him?"

"Hey!" Adrian smiled. "I'm an angel! I can do anything!"

"If you can do anything, then stop the train," Magnolia said as he stood up. Adrian reached over and pulled the emergency cord. The train did not stop.

"What's the matter?" Adrian asked, tugging on the cord again and again.

"Nothing," Magnolia said sweetly, pulling the cord himself. This time the train lurched to a halt. "Just a little reminder that you can't do everything. You boys have a nice day."

Adrian pulled the car into a strip mall off a busy highway, driving slowly past the large grocery store, the drugstore, the Laundromat, and Luigi's Pizza. The last storefront was a nondescript affair identified only by the letters *MEE* painted in yellowish green on the tinted front window. Adrian pulled into a parking spot directly in front of it.

"We're not going in there," Al said, casting a suspicious eye at Adrian.

"Yes, actually we are." Adrian turned off the car. As he did so, a middle-aged couple, each dressed in a garish yellow-green leotard that matched the colors of the MEE sign, came sprinting happily out of the store.

"You've got to be kidding," Al said. "Isn't this one of those Eastern religion meditation Hare-Krishna-dance-around-in-a-toga-with-a-bald-head kind of places? What could this possibly have to do with Dick Lynn and John G. Erie?"

"Trust me." Adrian patted him on the shoulder.

They walked into the store and were immediately greeted by the smell of an unpleasantly acrid incense and the soft chords of a sitar, slowly playing in accompaniment to a barely audible chant. Two men stood behind the counter, one completely bald and the other with contrastingly long, flowing hair. Neither was a particularly attractive man, each made less so by the yellow-green leotard bluntly accentuating his lack of physical toning. The bald man smiled and bowed slightly.

"Are you here to join MEE?"

"I didn't know you'd come apart," Al cracked.

The bald man laughed. "I don't mean me," he said, pointing to himself. "I mean MEE!" He pointed to the extended sign running across the wall above the lobby desk, which read, "Movement for

Existential Elevation." The bald man smiled broadly and pointed his index fingers at Al and Adrian. "Are you ready to change your life with MEE!"

"That's what my wife asked the day I got married," Al cracked again. He was finding it very difficult to take this seriously, although Adrian seemed to be doing just that.

"Here we take the reality of your existence, and we elevate it to a whole new plane." The bald man closed his eyes. "When you have attained this higher plane, you learn how to exist as one with the universe, where it matters not who you know, what you're worth, or what you have done." He opened his eyes and smiled peacefully. "You will attain an inner satisfaction that comes from the realization of your own self-worth and the worth of every other person." As the bald man spoke, the long-haired man closed his eyes and began a loud, monotonous chant.

"That guy must be one with a parallel universe," Al said quietly to Adrian.

"You can joke, my friend," the bald man said to Al, "but MEE is the fastest-growing franchise in America today. We are going to take the country by storm!"

"Somebody better tell Luigi next door," Al said to Adrian. "They'll be first to see hostile action."

"Will you be quiet?" Adrian snapped.

The bald man began to focus on the more seriously interested Adrian.

"We obviously reject such things as status . . . power . . . money," he continued.

"Really?" Al cut in. "If I offer to buy a membership, you'll reject my money?"

"We require funds to operate our parlor, sir," the bald man said patiently. "Membership is $59.95 for one year or $109.95 for two years. In addition to the membership fee, there is also a $14.95 charge for our book, which guides you through the courses." The bald man produced two wrapped pairs of leotards from beneath the counter. "You would also need a pair of these to wear to every meeting. They go for $24.95 each. I'll give you both pairs for $40." He pulled the leotards out of the plastic packages and held them up proudly.

"Why do we need to wear these at the meetings?" Adrian asked.

"Because the relaxation they provide ensures a pure state of meditation . . . which we call MEEditation."

"Forty dollars for a couple of leotards?" Al said to Adrian. "Please!"

"These aren't leotards. We call them MEEotards."

"We put those on, we'll look like REEotards." Al waved his hand in disgust.

Adrian ignored him and pulled out a wad of cash. "Sign us up for one year each." Adrian grabbed the MEEotards.

"You're just in time for the five o'clock meeting." The bald man handed them their books and gratefully took Adrian's cash. "Go through the door and you will be in our common MEEditation room. To the left you'll find dressing rooms. Put on your MEEotards and then join us in the common room."

Adrian led the way into the MEEditation room, where about two dozen people, all wrapped in MEEotards, were on the floor, lying on their sides in different states of meditation.

"Looks like a guacamole dip convention," Al said.

"Get changed." Adrian pushed him into the first changing stall, where Al was confronted by a full-length reflection of himself in a large mirror.

"Bad enough I have to put this stupid thing on," Al called over the wall, "now I have to see myself in it."

"Quit complaining," Adrian called out from the adjoining stall.

"Do I have to take everything off?" Al asked.

"Of course," Adrian replied. "How can you attain a true state of MEEditation with your underwear on?"

Al undressed and slipped his feet into the MEEotard. "I haven't worn Dr. Denton's since the third grade!" he shouted over the wall, pulling the clinging fabric up and over his body. "Now I know how my school lunches felt," he said to himself as he zippered the MEEotard up his left side until it locked into a plastic clip under his armpit. He took a quick look in the mirror and cringed. "I look like *Night of the Living Banana,*" he said to Adrian as he emerged from the dressing room.

Adrian was waiting for him. "How do I look?" he asked.

"Like a walking mustard jar," Al replied.

They entered the MEEditation room just as the bald-headed man was asking everyone to get into their smaller groups. As people milled about the floor, Adrian pointed to one particular man standing in a corner. Two things made this man stand out—he was by far the oldest person in the room and he had an air of authority about him that was unmistakable.

"Recognize the man with the silver hair?" Adrian asked Al. "That is Colin MacMillian, the chairman of the board of Eastern Wireless Communications. He's the guy with the final say on hiring your friend Dick Lynn." Adrian politely pushed through the crowd until they were standing next to MacMillian.

"All right if we join your group?" Adrian asked MacMillian.

"Of course!" MacMillian beamed as he introduced himself. "Glad to have you with us. Shows open-mindedness and takes courage for you to be here."

"Takes more courage to wear these outfits," Al said, eliciting a laugh from MacMillian.

"You're the chairman of Eastern Wireless, aren't you?" Adrian asked. MacMillian nodded. "Fancy meeting a chairman here," Adrian said, shaking MacMillian's hand.

"I come here all the time. Swear by it. My secretary turned me on to this place. Then she turned my chief financial officer on and they ran away together. But I keep coming here. This is better than golf or tennis or a cigar bar. MEE helps me reach an incredibly peaceful place. A place that helps me make the tough decisions I have to make and then live with them afterward. Join us." MacMillian, ever the leader, urged his group to gather around him on the floor. He promptly introduced Al and Adrian and then delved right into their topic.

"Here is where we left the discussion last week," he began. "Scientists tell us that the universe is still expanding, still growing. The question for us to ponder is this: Does the universe represent infinity? Or does the space in which the universe expands represent infinity? Since there can only be one infinity, which is it? Let's ask our new friends for their views."

MacMillian turned to a reluctant Al. Cosmic questions were not his thing, but he knew he couldn't ignore the question or MacMillian's invitation to answer.

"I suppose it all comes down to communication," he replied. "After all, almost everything on this planet communicates in one way or another. Plants, vines, trees, the lowly mollusk at the bottom of the sea—they all communicate in one way or another and we should take that into account as we live our lives."

"An excellent thought!" MacMillian clapped his hands. "What Al is saying, friends, is that the size of the universe is meaningless without communication, and that communication is meaningless without an understanding of the size of the universe, right, Al?"

"Couldn't have said it better myself," Al bluffed.

MacMillian turned to Adrian. "What about you, my friend?"

Adrian looked pensive for a moment. "If the universe is expanding, then it is swallowing up space that may have once belonged to someone or something else. That tells us there are only two kinds of existence in the universe—swallowers and swallowees. We all have to decide whether we want to swallow or be swallowed." The people in MacMillian's circle were blown away by this and dropped prone on the floor. They began chanting and humming vigorously. As it became more intense, Al gave Adrian a get-me-out of-here glance.

"Excellent." MacMillian nodded at Adrian, impressed. "I don't know about anyone else, but that has certainly helped me."

The bald man, who had been working his way from group to group, made his way into the center of their circle. "It is time for MEEditation." He coaxed everyone back onto their feet and marched them in an obedient line to the back of the MEEditation room. There was another set of doors along the wall, similar to the ones for the dressing rooms. The bald man held the first door open and invited Al inside. Adrian and MacMillian watched from the open doorway. The room gave off a warm and relaxing fluorescent white light, the source of the light coming from under the wooden chair guards halfway up the walls of the room. A bookshelf sat under the chair guard along the far wall, stuffed with hardcover self-help books about MEE. An oversized bed covered in a white sheet was situated in the middle of the room. At the top of the bed was a small fixed pillow, with two triangularly shaped clear plastic fixtures sprouting from either end of the pillow. A night table with multicolored bottles stood next to the bed.

"Try it out," the bald man said to Al, indicating the bed. Al pressed on the mattress with his hands and then sat down.

"Pretty comfortable mattress," he said.

"It's not a mattress. It's a MEEtress." The bald man invited Al to lie down. "Two hundred and forty-five handmade tensile springs contour to your body and caress it as you rest, allowing for the highest level of MEEditation," the bald man recited. "It retails for $249.99, but for new members we offer a special . . . $219.95. You will also find a selection of lotions and fragrances on the night table. We invite you to use as many of them as you like. Also, a library of MEE books is available on the bookshelf. Each is $19.95, or if you like, you can open up a rental account with us and for $9.95 a month, you can rent an unlimited number of books."

"Just out of curiosity"—Al sat up—"who founded the MEE movement? Lord and Taylor?"

"Angus Day McCarthy," the bald man said reverently.

"I feel like I'm worshipping at Our Lady of the Warehouse Clearance Sale."

"Nothing of the kind." The bald man remained serene. "Our followers want to have the same wonderful peaceful feelings at home as they do when they come here. We want to give them every opportunity to do so. That's part of Angus Day McCarthy's philosophy."

"I've never heard of this guy McCarthy. Is he a priest or a monk or something?"

"No. He's a potato farmer in Idaho. He had a vision."

"I can see that," Al said, looking at the $29.95 price tag on each of the lotion bottles on the night table.

"Let us leave our friend to MEEditate." The bald man stepped toward the door.

"MEEditate about what?" Al asked.

"About whatever concerns you, or turns you on, or turns you off. Think about one thing. Any one thing you like. Concentrate on it—every aspect of it—until you find yourself on that higher plane of existence."

"How will I know when I'm there?"

"You'll know," the bald man said.

"It works for me," MacMillian said softly. "I concentrate on a particular problem from the office . . . one that I'm having difficulty with. I MEEditate until I hear a little voice that tells me what I should do." He looked sheepishly at the other man. "I call him Ralph. I know it sounds crazy, but it works!" The bald man patted MacMillian on the shoulder knowingly and led him and Adrian out of the room.

Al stretched out on the MEEtress. He had to admit it was incredibly comfortable. He checked out the pillow. It was fixed to the bed and immovable, and Al noticed a pattern of small holes in the middle of each of the plastic triangles like those of an earphone. He cautiously laid his head down; the weight of his head triggered sounds from the plastic triangles . . . first a gently falling rain and then a faint breeze gently rustling the leaves of a tree. Al closed his eyes.

"It is good to have you lie down with MEE," a feminine voice flowed through the speakers and into Al's ears as gently as the sound of the breeze. "Join MEE on a higher level of existence. Listen with MEE to the gentle sounds of life that invite us to this higher plane . . . the sound of rain . . . a baby's giggle . . . a violin concerto. All of these pleasing and relaxing sounds can be yours on this MEE CD for only $14.95." The violin played a pleasing tune. Al felt his eyelids getting heavy, his body going limp on the MEEtress.

Suddenly Al was somewhere else. It was a high-ceilinged courtroom, circa 1930. A pair of ceiling fans anchored to a support beam were trying to circulate the hot heavy air. Al was sitting at the defense table decked out in a wide-lapelled double-breasted suit fashionable to the time period. Adrian sat calmly next to him, similarly dressed. Al's ex-wife, Liz, sat in the first row behind the table, looking pensive in a plain brown housedress. The room was filled to overflowing, everything in black, white, or a shade of gray, including the witness box, where Al's favorite Roundabout horse, Night, stood in the full glory of its hand-painted finish. Night was alive—animated and agitated at the ongoing cross-examination being conducted by the dapper prosecutor, a sharply dressed man with slick-backed hair and a pencil-thin mustache.

"Isn't it true," the prosecutor shouted, "that you knowingly allowed the defendant to ride your back, knowing full well you could no longer support his weight adequately?" The horse hung its head, unwilling to make eye contact. "Is it true?" the prosecutor shouted again. A few of the jurors jumped at the shrillness of his tone.

"Yes," Night said reluctantly.

"And isn't it true that you were unable to stop when the ride came to a halt, throwing yourself off the ride, killing that man there." The prosecutor pointed at Al.

"The ride started to go too fast." Night shuddered.

"Is it true?" the prosecutor demanded at the top of his lungs. "Did you wind up killing this man?" The horse, growing more and more agitated, continued to shake its head in denial. The prosecutor bore in, sensing the kill. "May I remind the witness that it is under oath! I warn you, horse! Do not lie! And do not leave any horse patties on the witness chair!"

"All right! Yes!" Night shouted back melodramatically, causing an audible stir in the gallery. "It's all true!" The horse began to whinny with shame.

The unsympathetic prosecutor walked slowly toward the witness box, nodding with satisfaction. "You bet it's true."

"I'm sorry!" the horse insisted.

"You are sorry, all right," the prosecutor snarled self-righteously, leaning in close to Night. "This court has nothing but justifiable contempt for you." The prosecutor straightened up. "Get off the stand," he demanded. "You make me sick!"

The courtroom exploded at the prosecutor's words. Reporters bolted from the room; photographers crowded around the defense table and the witness stand; the blinding light of flashbulbs popping everywhere. Al looked for his wife through the chaos. She was still in her seat, sobbing into a handkerchief.

The courtroom was suddenly gone, everything washed away in an instant, except for Liz, still in the housedress, still crying. Only now they were sitting together inside the big-top tent of a circus. They were alone.

"We missed the show," she said to Al. "The clowns . . . the acrobats . . . the elephants. They're all gone. They will be folding up the tent shortly. I so wanted to see the circus. Something fun. Something that would make me laugh," she said mournfully.

Al was only a few feet from her, but no matter how many times he tried to slide closer, she remained the same distance away. There were shouts and the wrenching noise of heavy machinery coming from outside the tent. Suddenly the tent began to lift from the ground, causing a swirl of dirt and dust that whipped into Al's eyes.

"Wait!" Al shouted. "There are people in here!" Using his hands to protect his eyes, Al began to feel a tugging at his right shoulder. He managed to open one eye. Adrian was hovering over him. Al had moved from the prone position to sitting on the edge of the MEEtress.

"Wake up!" Adrian said. "We have work to do."

Al shook the cobwebs out of his head. "Man! That was amazing! I thought I was—"

"You went into a MEEditation pretty quick," Adrian said. "I don't know what you were MEEditating about, but you were standing up and sitting down and yelling about circus elephants." Al stood up, a bit unsteady. Adrian steadied him. "You all right?"

"Yeah. I feel like I just woke up from a deep sleep."

"That's MEEditation. They play some soothing sounds in your ears. You get comfortable on the bed. Next thing you know . . . Whammo! You're MEEditating! Mr. MacMillian is MEEditating as we speak. We have to go see him while he's still under."

"Why? What can we do while he's MEEditating?"

"Make sure he has a conversation with Ralph." Adrian winked.

Adrian eased open the MEEditation room door next to Al's. MacMillian was motionless on the bed, his head fixed between the plastic triangles of his pillow. He was humming along to the chords of music they recognized as the *1812 Overture.*

"How are you going to do this?" Al whispered. Adrian put his finger to his lips, urging Al to be silent. Moving slowly, Adrian bent over the bed until he was almost directly over MacMillian's face. Suddenly the room filled with the explosive sound of MacMillian singing the chorus of the overture at the top of his lungs.

"Ta-ta-ta, ta-ta-ta-ta, ta-ta-ta, taaaaaaa . . ." MacMillian sat up as he held the last note. Adrian was quick enough to dive under the bed and out of view, but Al froze in place as MacMillian's eyes lasered in on him.

"Stand fast, men!" MacMillian commanded, throwing his hands authoritatively on his hips. "Since the Little Emperor has seen fit to defile our homeland, then he shall have our answer with cannon and sword!" MacMillian pantomimed as though drawing a sword from a scabbard at his waist. He held his arm high and moved toward Al. "Look sharp, men! Here comes the first wave of cavalry!" Al tried to back away, but MacMillian, sensing his movement, turned, a disturbing frenzy in his eyes. "Let no man shirk in his duty to his country at this critical time! Show them the cold steel!"

"Take out your sword!" Adrian told Al from beneath the bed.

"I don't have one!" Al answered back in a strained whisper.

"Neither does he, but that's not stopping him, is it? Pretend!"

Al repeated MacMillian's pantomime and pulled an imaginary sword from his waist.

"Ready, General!" he said. MacMillian looked at him quizzically, then turned and rushed to the other side of the bed. He turned and fixed another glare on Al again.

"There's the Little Emperor!" he shouted angrily, pointing what was supposed to be his sword at Al.

"What is this Little Emperor stuff?" Al asked, making a move toward the bed.

"Stay up where you are! Let him see you!" Adrian urged. "He thinks you're Napoleon."

"Napoleon Bonaparte?" Al asked incredulously.

"No. Jerry Bonaparte, the plumber from Queens New York."

Suddenly MacMillian rushed around the bed and grabbed Al angrily.

"You'll not do this to my people, you cur!" MacMillian shouted, his surprisingly powerful arms wrapping Al in a viselike headlock. Al tried to resist, but he didn't have the leverage, as MacMillian was violently bouncing his head up and down.

"Is this any way to treat the ruler of France?" Al demanded.

"Shush! You might wake him up!" Adrian said from beneath the bed.

"I can't take much more of this!" Al warned.

"Hey! Remind me when we're done. I'll introduce you to Napoleon if you want. Not a bad little short guy! A little stubborn . . . great memory . . . moody sometimes . . . good sense of humor if you catch him on the right day."

As Adrian finished, Al finally squeezed his head out of MacMillian's grasp and fell backward to the floor. MacMillian grabbed at Al's waist.

"Stand him up in front of the firing squad, men!"

Al wriggled free and started crawling under the bed.

"Don't bring him down here!" Adrian blocked Al from getting under the bed.

"Nice friend you are! Didn't you hear him? He wants to put me in front of a firing squad! I'll be Napoleon Blownaparte!"

In that instant, MacMillian stopped struggling with Al and gently sat himself on the edge of the bed.

"Ilsa!" he called gently. "Ilsa!" he repeated, looking romantically at Al.

"Who's Ilsa?" Al asked Adrian, uncomfortable with the look he was getting from MacMillian. The chairman jumped off the bed and held out his hand to help Al up. Adrian nodded that he should take the hand. He did and MacMillian pulled him to his feet and began tenderly rubbing his shoulders.

"Here's looking at you, kid," he said warmly. "Ilsa, I'm no good at being noble, but it doesn't take much to see that the problems of three little people don't amount to a hill of beans in this crazy world. We both know you belong with Victor. If that plane leaves the ground and you're not with him, you'll regret it. Maybe not today. Maybe not tomorrow, but soon and for the rest of your life."

"Hey!" Al brightened. "That's from *Casablanca*. He thinks I'm Ingrid Bergman!"

"God! Wait until he wakes up and finds you look more like Ingmar Bergman."

MacMillian was looking deep into Al's eyes and began pulling him closer.

"Okay! This is far enough!" Al said to MacMillian, beginning to resist. "Adrian, do something. I am not going to kiss this guy!"

"Colin!" Adrian called softly from under the bed. "Colin! It's me! Ralph!" MacMillian looked pleased and relieved.

"What took you so long to get here today?" MacMillian asked, letting go of Al.

"Sorry. But I'm here now. Lie down, Colin. Relax."

"Did you give any more thought to what we talked about last

week?" MacMillian asked as he sat down on the MEEtress and swung his feet up on the bed obediently.

"I did," Adrian bluffed. "Did you?"

"Yes, I did. I thought about how I go to the office every day. I see hundreds, maybe thousands, of people in the hallways, in the cafeteria, in the parking lot, and many of them go out of their way to say hello to me . . . not because they like me . . . not because I'm their friend . . . but because I'm the boss. And I look at all of these people knowing that every decision I make impacts their careers and livelihoods. I used to love that feeling. I wanted to be the general and lead the troops into battle and win a big victory. But a lot of days lately, I feel like I just want to stay home with my wife and watch old movies . . . read the paper . . . sit on the front porch. And I ask myself, 'How can I be a good leader if I only want to lead on certain days? How can I be a good leader if there are days when all I want to do is stay home and watch *Casablanca*?'"

"You know what a good leader does?" Adrian asked as he pulled himself out from under the bed and stood up. MacMillian's eyes were closed tightly and his relaxed body indicated he had achieved MEEditation. "A good leader surrounds himself with strong subordinates and sometimes he lets them lead the charge into battle. A good leader has strong lieutenants so he can establish a succession plan, preventing chaos when he leaves."

"I agree, Ralph." MacMillian nodded.

"Good. Surround yourself with good leaders, Colin."

"I do."

"There is a man you met the other day who is a good leader. His name is Dick Lynn."

"Yes, I remember. I was impressed."

"Hire him! Go into the office tomorrow and call your personnel people and tell them before they do anything else to call Dick Lynn and hire him into the company. You can never have too many leaders."

"I will do that, Ralph," MacMillian said. "That's very good. I feel better already. And you know what? The other big problem we talked about last week. I've reached a decision on that one, too. I was talking to a man today who said something very profound . . . that everything in the universe is either a swallower or a swallowee. And that's when it hit me. For Eastern Wireless to survive, we must be a swallower!"

"Good, Colin. It sounds like you're ready to go out there and lead your troops again!" Adrian led Al quietly to the door. "Happy MEEditating!" he said as he shut the door behind them.

Richard Lynn was hired by Eastern Wireless Communications a week later, and two weeks after that, he stood on a stage with MacMillian and other executives from Eastern Wireless Communications as well as executives from LoonaTechnologies, facing a large audience of reporters, which included Al and Adrian in the last row.

"We have been weighing the merits of this deal for a while," MacMillian said. "And it comes down to this. In this world, you either swallow or be swallowed. To survive, you must swallow. Eastern Wireless is a swallower, and that is why today we announced proudly that we have bought LoonaTechnologies."

The press conference went on for thirty minutes, with the head of LoonaTech following MacMillian and, with a forced enthusiasm, explaining why this was a great opportunity for his company as well.

Then, after some questions from the press, the meeting adjourned.

"I feel very good for Dick." Al beamed. "Thank you for helping him, Adrian. I mean that."

"There's one more thing you'll like." Adrian beckoned Al to follow him. Among the groups of people still chatting in the room were MacMillian with Lynn and a glum-looking John G. Erie.

"No reflection on you, John," MacMillian was saying. "But I want my own man in charge of the company's marketing and communications. So Dick Lynn will be in charge and you will report to him. You fellows work out the details. Thank you." Smiling, MacMillian joined another small group of executives.

"We need to get together tomorrow and start planning the merging of the two groups," Dick said.

"I'm free in the afternoon," Erie said reluctantly.

"I'm not," Dick said, enjoying every moment of this. "I'm free in the morning. Change your schedule. I'll see you at nine o'clock."

"Okay," Erie said, obviously resigned to the situation. "I would like a couple of minutes to tell you all the good things we've initiated within our group," Erie said tentatively.

"Not necessary," Dick snapped back. "I'm not going to focus on the past. Only the future."

Erie's shoulders slumped.

"Listen, Dick," he said out of range of the other executives. "I hope we can be professional about this." Dick paused a moment, then broke out into a big grin.

"Not a chance," Dick said, and walked away.

CHAPTER 15

the fifth jerk al mitchell meets on earth

BULL SHOALS LAKE rests in north-central Arkansas, formed when the U.S. Army Corps of Engineers erected the fifth-largest concrete dam in the United States along the White River shortly after World War II. The dam provides much-needed power to what is still an out-of-the-way area and also regulates the flow of millions of gallons of water into the Lower White River Basin and its fingerlike tributaries, which run for hundreds of miles north and west into Missouri. Bull Shoals sits in a basin surrounded by the stern southern tier of the Ozark Mountains, giving the lake area a rugged complexion and an austerity born from its isolation.

"This is where the serious fisherman comes." Adrian stood on a limestone rock jutting out of a hill over the lake surface. "The nicer-looking places, like the California Sierras, the Adirondacks, they're like Disneyland . . . always crowded . . . strictly for tourists. Bull Shoals is the real thing. You can go out on your boat for hours here and not see another person. All you'll see are fish just lining up to be caught."

"I was never much on fishing." Al picked up a stone and, keeping a safe distance from the edge of the rock, tossed it into the water. "I see a fish in the water, I think of Charlie the Tuna or Boss Barracuda . . . or *Finding Nemo*. Besides, I don't like a sport where you don't keep score."

"Fishing is a different mind-set, Al. It's not about the competition. It's about enjoying a good moment in life." Adrian closed his eyes and took in as much of the Ozark air as he could. "You sit on your boat on a sunny day with the fresh air in your face, the lake as smooth as glass, quiet as a whisper. You can hear nature talk to you, in a raw, unbridled way, letting you in on some of the secrets she keeps from folks who don't have time to hear what she has to say." Adrian walked to the edge of the rock and leaned forward until he was almost completely off it. Al thought at any moment Adrian was going to shout that he was "the king of the world."

"I came here a lot after the war and this was a special place to me," he reflected. "Look how blue that water is." Al took a halting couple of steps toward the edge of the rock and stretched his neck to see over the side. The drop was twenty or thirty feet. Adrian was amused by Al's caution.

"Hey, Al! Watch this!" he said, planting his feet firmly on the very edge of the rock, then allowing himself to slowly fall forward like the drawbridge of a castle until he was parallel with the surface of the rock, seemingly held up by nothing but air. "Try it!" he urged Al.

"No thanks," Al said glumly.

"There's nothing to worry about! You won't get hurt!"

"I know." Al kicked loose a group of small pebbles from the rock and picked them up. "If it's all the same to you, I'd rather not." Adrian returned to an upright position as Al began gently tossing the pebbles over one by one, watching the ripples from his ultrasafe perch.

"Having a reflective moment, are we?" Adrian asked.

"I know this is going to sound funny"—Al tossed the last of his pebbles—"but it just sunk in that I'm really dead. I've been so busy since I met you, I guess I hadn't thought about it until just now, when I realized I was in no danger on this rock."

"It happens to everybody," Adrian said.

"Seeing Dick Lynn reminded me of how much my job meant to me. Seeing Liz in my MEEditation moment reminded me that I always thought I would get the chance to fix things with her. But I never did." Al picked up two bigger rocks and flung the first to the water with more animation. "I wanted to write a book. Visit the North Pole. Do a lot of other damn things." He whipped the second rock into the water angrily. "How come my life had to be so damn short!" he shouted purposely, so he could hear the words echo off of the surrounding peaks.

"Don't start talking about that," Adrian cautioned quietly. "It's not appropriate."

"Why?" challenged Al, getting visibly agitated. "How many years did you live?"

"Fifty-five."

"That's ten more than me!" he said angrily, kicking at a loose pebble and sending it flying to the lake below. Al was suddenly feeling tired, frustrated . . . replaying that fatal fling on that stupid horse. His anger was welling up and he could no longer suppress it. "It's not fair. Dammit!" He stormed off the rock toward the woods a short way down a crumbling rock path.

"Where are you going?" Adrian called out. "We have to finish!"

"I don't want to finish!" Al shouted without turning around.

"You don't have a choice!" Adrian whipped out the words as he darted in front of Al. "You don't just walk away from HARP!"

"Watch me." Al slipped around Adrian and kept walking. "I've had enough!" Adrian moved quickly in front of Al again.

"Stop this!" Now Adrian was getting annoyed. "You and I have more HARPing to do!"

"Do it yourself!" Al snapped, pushing Adrian to the side, knocking him off balance. Adrian regained his footing quickly and grabbed Al's arm.

"Let go!" Al demanded through a clenched jaw. He tried to wrest his arm free, but Adrian refused to lighten his grip. They continued their tug-of-war.

"Not until we're done!"

"Go to hell!" Al seethed.

The words ignited a blinding rage in Adrian, and the angel violently grabbed Al by the shoulder, turned him around, and pushed him to the ground with an explosive two-handed shove.

"Don't you dare say that to me!" he screamed as Al had never heard another person, living or otherwise, scream before. Al hit the ground hard, but fortunately his head hit a soft spot of dirt. Adrian stepped over the stunned Al, straddling him as he pulled out his

HEAVEN box with a shaking pair of hands. "You think you have something to complain about?" He opened the box and shoved the screen in Al's face. "Look at these!" he commanded. One by one, pictures flashed on the screen like a slide show, each one a young child: the first bald and pale; the second with a respirator mask covering a deathly white face; the third on a hospital bed, hooked to a respirator; the fourth a skeletal shadow of a young girl. "Would you like me to introduce you to a couple of these kids? Not one of them saw their tenth birthday."

"Okay, stop," Al cut him off, his voice a remorseful whisper.

"No! I won't stop!" Adrian pulled out a frayed black-and-white photograph from the pocket of his jacket. "Let me ask you something, Al. What were you doing on your nineteenth birthday?"

"I don't remember."

"Let me refresh your memory. You were doing the same thing millions of nineteen-year-old boys do on their birthday. You were getting drunk with your college friends. They threw you a party in Fort Lauderdale."

Al tried not to smile at the memory. "Oh yeah . . . I remember . . . at least some of it."

"This is my brother." Adrian pushed the photo in Al's face. A high-cheeked boy standing proudly in his service uniform smiled back at Al. "On his nineteenth birthday he landed with the Fourth Marine Division on Iwo Jima! He didn't survive the landing." Adrian stood up straight and finally corralled his temper. He took a look at the picture, regretting the wrinkles he had put in it with his angry, tightfisted grip. He laid the photo flat in his left hand and ran his right hand over it like an iron. The wrinkles disappeared. Adrian placed the picture carefully back into his pocket and closed the HEAVEN box.

"Now tell me again how unfair your life was!" he said, subdued.

He walked back onto the limestone rock.

"I'm sorry," Al called out. Adrian kept his back to him, looking out over the vista of the lake. "I'm just not used to being dead."

"Get used to it," Adrian responded unsympathetically.

℮ Al stood and brushed himself off. The way his head had hit the ground, he expected a headache or neck pain or something . . . but he felt fine. He wasn't sure what set him off or why, but it was time to make amends with Adrian. He joined Adrian at the edge of the rock.

"Are you talking to me?" Al asked. Adrian ignored him.

"I said I was sorry." Adrian remained silent. Al suddenly turned to Adrian and folded his hands as if in prayer.

"Tell me you forgive me or I'll jump!" he said in a mock melodramatic tone, looking to the lake below. He waited, but Adrian still gave no hint of a response. "It's a long way down . . . a life-threatening drop!"

"Go ahead . . . jump," Adrian said with no concern in his voice. "A dead man can't kill himself."

"Okay . . . so it's an afterlife-threatening drop . . . at least it is hypothetically speaking."

Adrian again did not react.

"Okay . . . maybe not hypothetically speaking . . . maybe I'm speaking like a large needle. That would be hypo-dermically speaking." Al nudged an implacable Adrian in the ribs. "How about if I was always thinking I was sick while I was talking? What would I be?" A stoic Adrian continued to gaze silently ahead. "Hypochondriacally speaking!" Al shouted, giving Adrian an emphatic "Ta-da!" but still to no reaction. "Of course, I could talk without the pollen blocking up my nose, and I'd be hypo-allergenically speaking." Nothing from Adrian. "Come on, Adrian! Work with me here!" Al pleaded. "I could talk while my body is becoming too cold to function. What would I be then?"

"Speaking hypo-thermically," Adrian replied in an unamused monotone.

"Right!" Al rubbed his chin. "And if I was speaking like a very heavy short-legged mammal that likes to hang around by the water hole, I would be . . ."

Adrian frowned, not sure of this one.

"Hypo-potamusly speaking!"

Adrian finally turned to Al and did all he could not to smile.

"That was really stupid!"

"Come on! Adrian! Where's your sense of humor! This is funny stuff!"

"You have a universally distorted definition of *funny.*" Adrian's cool was finally melted.

"I am sorry!" Al repeated one more time.

Adrian took Al by the arm much more gently than before.

"Here's a warning for you, Al. Telling an angel to go to hell is not smart. It's like telling a Hatfield to go have dinner with the McCoys."

"I guess I got a little frustrated about having my life end on a merry-go-round. I'm sorry I lost my temper." He offered his hand.

"Okay." Adrian extended his hand as well, but at the last second Al pulled his hand back.

"Nobody shakes hands in heaven, remember?"

"Very funny," Adrian said. "You realize you are standing on the edge of the rock. It doesn't bother you anymore?"

"Nope. It's a nice view."

"Why don't you try doing what I did before? You'll get even a better view."

Al gave Adrian a why-not look and stood straight up, his feet at the edge of the rock. He slowly started over just as Adrian had, but instead of a slow drop, he just pitched forward and plummeted to the water below. His scream was quickly drowned out by the huge splash. After a few moments, Al's head bobbed back to the surface.

"What happened?" he called up to Adrian. "What did I do wrong?"

"Nothing." Adrian shrugged casually. "You can't do what an angel can do until you get full rights and privileges."

"I thought you said I wouldn't fall?" Al shouted back.

"I said you wouldn't get hurt! Are you hurt?"

"No."

"See? I was right!"

℃ Adrian was sitting on the limestone rock, his eyes fixed on the HEAVEN box opened on his lap, when Al emerged from the trees, sopping wet.

"Not very good form on that dive, Al," said Adrian. "Personally, I'd give you a 9.3, but I'm known to be lenient. You're lucky there's no East Germany anymore. East German judge would have given you a 6.5 . . . maybe worse." Adrian indicated Al should sit next to him. "While you were splashing around in the lake, I got a head start on your ex-wife." He showed Al a flattering picture of Liz on the screen.

"Why are you looking at my ex-wife?"

"I was assuming she was your fifth jerk."

"No. It's not her."

"Really?" Adrian looked almost bewildered, crestfallen. "Every person we have ever had in HARP identified an ex-spouse as a jerk. How can you not?"

"Don't get me wrong . . . I had more than my share of differences with Liz. But when I'm honest with myself—which seems to be a lot easier to do since I died—I can't blame her for our breakup."

"Maybe it's for the best." Adrian sighed. "We were starting to have a problem with people who were divorced two or three times. . . . They wanted to HARP on all their ex-spouses. We're looking to discourage that. So we're putting a rule in place that sets a limit of two ex-spouses as jerks."

"Why?"

"We're protecting the program for when Liz Taylor gets up here." Adrian pushed a button and Al's wife dissolved away. "Now you've got me curious. Who is your fifth jerk?"

"I don't know his name."

"How can you not know his name if he was such a jerk to you?"

"I want to HARP on the maintenance guy for the Seafarer Beach Roundabout."

Adrian was taken aback. "You want to HARP the maintenance man? *THAT's* your fifth jerk?" Adrian looked troubled.

"He got me killed!" Al snapped, responding to Adrian's obviously negative reaction.

"I know. But other than that, he's an okay guy."

"Gee, I'm glad to hear that. Maybe you'd like to nominate him for sainthood," Al said indignantly.

"He's not a killer, Al. Killers premeditate. Killers use knives and guns and poison. You think the maintenance guy premeditated this?"

"I don't know."

"You think he woke up and said, 'Okay, today's the day I get Al Mitchell! Break out my double-barreled shotgun . . . nah, too loud. Maybe I could show his insides my new never-needs-sharpening steak knife . . . nah, too messy. I know! I'll take him out with my nefarious merry-go-round.'"

"He was responsible." Al repeated, unmoved.

"You could say the same thing about the ride operator or the guy who wrote the software for the computer that controlled the ride."

"I want the maintenance guy!" Al insisted.

Adrian sighed and pushed a few buttons on the HEAVEN box.

"Okay. If that's your choice, I have to go along with it. The guy's name is Chester Harbourton." Al held up the open screen. Here, look . . ."

Present Day

Chet Harbourton, black and about forty, had to lay his tall, wiry frame diagonally across his rumpled bed in order to fit. A cold compress lay across his forehead, partially covering his white-streaked hair. A ghostly sliver of light coming from under the bedroom door reflected the mix of sweat and tears on his face. The only parts of his body that moved were his hands rolling through the beads of the rosary and his lips, which continued to silently repeat the Hail Marys. There was a loud banging on the door, but he ignored it in favor of the prayers he continued to recite.

"Chet!" a voice called out loudly, and then repeated more softly, as if trying to coax a response. "Chester! Come out and have something to eat. Dinner is ready."

"I'm not hungry," Chet rasped between "The Lord is with thee" and "Blessed art thou . . ."

"You have to eat! It's been three days!"

"No. Not tonight," he said at the end of the prayer.

"Your children are begging you to come out!"

The thought of his distraught children was too painful. How could he ever explain to them what he had done? He began reciting the next set of prayers more intensely. Where was the comfort the priest always said would come from the Almighty with prayer?

"Chester Harbourton!" The voice behind the door was more insistent. "You have to stop blaming yourself for what happened! The police said it was an accident! The investigators said it was an accident! Witnesses said it was an accident! The insurance company said it was an accident, and you know they wouldn't say it if it wasn't true!"

"I know what they say"—Chet let go of the rosary and brought his hands up to his face—"but they ain't the man who was on that ride. What would he say?"

He covered his face and began to cry.

Adrian closed the HEAVEN box.

"I'm not supposed to influence your decisions either way,"

Adrian said. "But look at this guy. He's wracked with guilt. He hasn't slept in three days."

"Gee, it's nice to know that my life is worth at least three sleepless nights," Al said bitterly. "Why were you so willing to help me with the first four jerks, but this jerk you want to give a free pass?"

"Because the other jerks were jerks, Al! They were selfish! They were out for themselves! They had no moral compass. You were right to call them jerks. But this guy . . ." Adrian shook his head. "When you call Chester Harbourton a jerk, you are as wrong as you can be."

"Easy for you to say, Adrian. He didn't kill you."

"You have to stop being angry about being dead. It happens to the best of us."

"I'm not angry!" Al's tone belied his words.

"Then see Chet Harbourton for what he is!" Adrian came back with equal force. "He holds two jobs. He's a maintenance man at the boardwalk. He's a full-time carpenter. He supports his wife, four kids, and a sick mother. He served in the Gulf War. He does volunteer work at his church every other weekend."

"I just think the guy owes me," Al said, his tone more measured.

"Suppose he does owe you, Al. How are you going to make him pay? He's distraught . . . near the edge. If we HARP on him, even in jest, it might put him over the edge. He could have a breakdown . . . do something nasty to himself . . . maybe to others. And that could be a bigger problem than you think."

"Why?"

"Because if we do something to change Chet Harbourton's course of life, the outcome will not be pleasant for any of us." Adrian invited Al to look at the HEAVEN box again.

Next Year

*The summer boardwalk looked its finest . . . bright
sunlight, shimmering blue ocean, happy families running from attraction to attraction. A particularly large
crowd had gathered at the end of the boardwalk near
Maxie's, where a billboard promised a never-before-
seen thrill of a lifetime! Underneath was a huge photograph of two gorillas with computer-enhanced smiles
on their faces. Large red letters above their heads proclaimed the coming of a new amphitheater and the east
coast debut of Butch and Sundance, the world's only
pair of diving gorillas.*

*Chet was in the meeting when the promoter, a baldish
nearing-seventy-year-old Florida man in an orange leisure
suit and garish yellow shirt explained his can't-miss act
to the Seafarer Boardwalk Management Association.*

*"Two adult gorillas take an elevator up to the diving
platform a hundred feet in the air over a swimming
pool," he said excitedly, acting it all out with manic
hand movements. "The lights in the amphitheater dim
and we see the film clip from* Butch Cassidy and the
Sundance Kid *where they decide to jump off the cliff
into the river below. Only, when Butch and Sundance
decide to do the jump, the screen suddenly goes black
and the two gorillas do the jump instead!"*

*Chet wondered what kind of man wakes up one morn-
ing and decides for his life's work, he is going to train
gorillas to dive into swimming pools. It was the craziest*

idea Chet had ever heard, which was probably why, one month later, the boardwalk was building the amphitheater.

Chet was on duty the day the act debuted to a full house. The gorillas were riding up the open-platform elevator when one of them started to act distressed. Having been given the responsibility to keep an eye on the elevator and its furry cargo, Chet noticed a light beaming right into the eyes of the flustered gorilla. He traced the light downward to its source. A woman almost directly under the diving platform—a young model-like beauty—had her right hand up to her ear, holding a cell phone, unaware the large diamond ring on her finger was reflecting the stage lights upward. As the elevator slowed, the agitated gorilla started jumping and raising its arms. The audience reacted with laughter, thinking it was part of the show, but Chet had the notion the gorilla, once out of the elevator, would lunge to grab at the stream of light, and if it lunged too much, the crowd under the platform would have the surprise of a thousand-pound gorilla bomb. Thinking quickly, Chet rushed to the woman's seat and convinced her to shut down her phone, in time to calm the primate.

Adrian pushed a button on the HEAVEN box and the picture of the woman with the cell phone froze in place.

"Chet was right about the gorilla. It would have fallen trying to grab at the light. The poor thing would have landed right on this lady. Chet saved this lady and a bunch of others from seeing the wrong side of a falling monkey."

"You want me to leave Chet Harbourton alone so he can prevent some lady from being used as a diving board by King Kong?" Al asked.

"That would be a terrible fate," Adrian said.

"Maybe I should let her be crushed. Then you could laugh at her when she gets up here." Al began imitating Adrian's voice, "Oh . . . ha-ha-ha . . . maybe we should notify the police. . . . If you see this gorilla, take no action yourself. Maybe we could feature the gorilla on *America's Most Wanted*. Or write a book. Call it *Le Morte de Monkey*.

Adrian laughed heartily. "Pretty funny, there, Al. But you don't understand my point. This lady that Chet saves is pretty important. She's an aspiring actress. Her name is Flora Enfawna. After Chet saves her life, she goes on to meet and marry a man named Angus Day McCarthy."

"The guy from MEE?" Al asked unbelievingly.

"One and the same. Now here's the payoff, Al. Flora meets McCarthy, becomes a successful actress, and persuades McCarthy to move from his potato farm in Idaho to Hollywood. He becomes a pretty successful agent and the MEE movement fizzles out."

"Sounds like a happy ending."

"But . . . if Chet doesn't save Flora, and she isn't around to meet McCarthy . . ." Adrian shuddered. "Look for yourself."

Further in the Future

The screen blinked to a shot of the Empire State Building, the Sears Tower, the Washington Monument, and the St. Louis Gateway Arch, all with huge MEE

*banners hanging from them. Then to a happy portrait of
Angus Day McCarthy, standing in Walt Disney World,
surrounded by the usual gaggle of cartoon characters,
waving to dozens of surrounding admirers. He was
holding a huge pair of scissors in his hand.*

*"I now declare the one-thousandth MEE parlor
open!" McCarthy called out giddily as the crowd
roared its approval and he cut the ribbon fronting a
MEE parlor in the middle of Disney World's Main
Street. A news narrator began a voice-over on the film.*

*"The crowd shouts its enthusiastic support for Angus
Day McCarthy, the founder and grand master of the
MEE movement as he opens his one-thousandth MEE
parlor, an amazing testimonial to an amazing man who
started as a potato farmer and had the spuds to follow
his dream. Starting with one MEE parlor in an abandoned potato-peeling mill in Boise, Idaho, McCarthy
mashed the competition and turned MEE into a national
movement with fifty million followers, including the
president and half the U.S. Congress; a prime-time TV
show five nights a week; two best-selling books; and a
MEEusement park covering over one thousand acres
in California! In the words of Angus Day McCarthy,
'There's nothing stopping MEE now!' MEEotards are
now the hottest-selling clothing item in the world,
MEEtresses are the sleep technology of choice, the
capital of Minnesota has officially changed its name
to MEEniapolis, and there is a growing movement to
rename the first planet in the solar system MEEcury!"*

The screen went blank. Adrian turned to Al.

"Do you really want to see fifty million Americans wearing those banana suits? How would your grandmother look in it? That fat Uncle Chuckie of yours? Butch Lowe?"

"It's too horrible for words," Al said.

"Flora Enfawna is the only person who can prevent it, and Chet Harbourton is the only person who can save her."

Al scratched his head and stared at the blank screen.

"Let me talk to Harbourton."

"That's against the rules. I can't do that."

"Come on, Adrian. When was the last time you lost sleep over bending some rules?" Adrian thought for a moment.

"Okay," he replied. "But you have to talk to someone else first."

"Who?" Al responded to the thin air, as Adrian had already whisked him away. Although he hadn't moved, he felt a bit dizzy and tried to get his bearings. Darkness suddenly turned to light. He was in the middle of a spacious, unattractive box of a building, rows and rows of trusses hanging from the ceiling above his head holding champagne-glass-shaped halogen lights that illuminated row after row of jukeboxes as far as Al's eye could see.

"Me!" a voice rang out from behind Al. "Adrian wanted you to talk to me."

Al turned to confront a behemoth of a man leaning casually with his elbow on top of a nearby jukebox. He straightened himself up with a playful guffaw, revealing a frame that had to be approaching seven feet tall, and a powerful build, although years of fat had overtaken the original muscles. He still had a pair of sharply square shoulders over which draped a red shirt that made him look like a walking brick wall. Al took an instinctive step backward as this chuckling freight train approached.

"Take it easy, man. I'm not going to eat you"—the man laughed and paused, grabbing Al's hand—"yet!" Now he burst into a resonant gut-busting laugh that echoed off the walls of the building and seemed to shake the jukeboxes. "Your name is Al, right? Well, don't worry, Al. I don't eat human beings . . . except on holidays. Hey! Come to think of it . . . isn't the Fourth of July coming up?" He let loose another foundation-shaking laugh. "My name is . . . or at least it was Frank Maye. Maybe you heard of me on earth."

Al shook his head apologetically.

"Never heard of me?" The big man frowned, disappointed. "Then I will eat you!" he roared, taking a threatening step toward Al, who backed off like a scared kitten. Frank broke into another chorus of laughs and threw a meat hook of an arm affectionately around Al. The laughter seemed so genuine, it was infectious. Al began chuckling, too. "I was a pro wrestler. Frankie T. Mayhem, they called me! I was pretty good, too; won half the tag team championship belt once."

"What happened to the other half?" Al said cautiously. "You eat it?"

Frank laughed hysterically again; the up-and-down heaves of his body were bobbing Al up and down like he was in a blender.

"Adrian told me you were a funny guy!" Frank said, still giggling. "In case you haven't noticed by now, I like to laugh. I think that's why they gave me this job."

"What job?" Al took a needed breath as Frank loosened his hug.

"I run a program that helps people get rid of their anger once and for all."

"I'm not angry!" A frustrated Al threw his hands in the air. "And I don't need a stupid anger management program."

"This isn't anger management." Frank smiled pleasantly. "If all you do is manage your anger, then you still have it. My program gets rid of your anger . . . because you can't be angry in heaven. I call the program Mandatory Anger Dissipation—MAD. I came up with the slogan for the program all by myself. You want to hear it?"

"Something tells me I don't have a choice."

"Get MAD so you don't get angry! How's that?"

"Very clever."

"And how do you like my jukeboxes? You got to smash one of them when you first got here, remember? That's one of my ideas, too. Let people work out their anger physically. It works for most people. I guess it didn't work for you."

"It worked for me," Al insisted. Frank put his arm around Al again, much more gently this time, and led him on a walk between the jukeboxes.

"Al, you're not the only one who has issues after dying. Some people have anxiety over the loved ones they left behind . . . especially parents when they leave their kids. Some people go into a kind of shock because the transition they have to make from mortality to immortality is rough. You know, one day there is a beginning and an end, then the next day there is no beginning or end. It can be disconcerting. Others are angry over something about their life. It's more normal than you think."

"I'm fine," Al insisted. "I was just a little frustrated about my life ending so early."

Frank brought them to a halt.

"What makes you think your life ended early? What makes you think you didn't get every minute that was coming to you?"

Al was taken back a bit by the question.

"I just assumed because it was an accident. . . ."

"Don't assume," Frank urged, his manner still warm and friendly. "Despite what you might have seen, people up here do know what they're doing"—he winked—"most of the time. You got your forty-five years because that's all you were scheduled to have."

"Oh!" Al scratched his head. "I didn't think of it that way."

"A lot of people don't. Everybody thinks they're supposed to live to be a hundred and if they don't . . . then somebody up here screwed up. That's not the way it works. Besides, that's not why you're angry. I recognize your problem because I see it in people every day."

"Okay." Al resigned himself to the conversation. "What's my problem?"

"You're angry because you didn't make as much out of your life as you had hoped to." Frank squeezed Al's shoulder reassuringly. Frank reached into his pocket and pulled out his own HEAVEN box.

"I could stand here and recite a list of good things you did with your life. You had a productive career. You helped a lot of people in your profession. You donated a lot of money to children's hospitals, and you sponsored Christmas parties at your neighborhood schools. You even helped Dick Lynn get a new job after you were up here. But you knew all that already."

"That doesn't make up for everything I didn't do."

"Maybe not." Frank opened the HEAVEN box. "Remember your college baseball coach?"

"Marty Critten? Yeah. I never liked him much because of what he did to Gonzo Gonzalez."

"That wasn't his finest moment, I'll give you that. But he did tell you something important once. Remember your sophomore year on the team?"

"Awful." Al shuddered reliving the memories. "I stunk up every stadium we played in. Halfway through the season I was hitting .120."

"You were hitting .115," the big man whispered, "but who's counting? You remember the game against Sacramento? You struck out three times?"

"Yeah. Critten pinch-hit for me in the eighth inning."

"Then he called you into his office afterward?"

"I remember walking toward his office, thinking he's either benching me or throwing me off the team."

"He didn't do either, did he?" Frank held up the screen of his HEAVEN box.

May 1980

Marty Critten leaned back in his chair and kicked off his cleats as Al entered the room. Al nervously took the chair on the other side of the coach's desk. Critten pulled off his cap, which unleashed a mass of curly brown hair, and ran his hands through it—how that mane fit under the modest cap was anyone's guess.

"Another tough day, huh, kid?" Critten said, putting his stocking feet up on the table.

"I know I stunk again today, Coach," Al began to

explain, "but I'm seeing the ball well. I just have to work on—"

"Take it easy, kid," Critten said. "You need to calm down. And I don't mean in here. I mean out on the field. Look, kid, I don't know if you're a good player or a great player, but I know you're better than you've shown so far. You need to stop worrying about yesterday's game. Every time you have a bad game, you try that much harder the next day. You're trying to get five hits every time you come to the plate to make up for not getting a hit yesterday. What you need to do is take a deep breath and tell yourself that the first half of the season is gone and you can't get it back. What you need to do is focus on having a great second half. If you do that, you and everybody else will forget about the first half."

"I hit over .300 in the second half." Al smiled. "He was right about that."

"And what you need to do now, Al, is focus on your time coming up in the afterlife . . . not on what is over and done with. Do the same thing now you did in your sophomore year."

"Okay," a subdued Al replied. "I get the point."

"Good. I think you really do." Frank closed the HEAVEN box. "A little help!" he cried out at the top of his lungs. The cherub that Al met when he first got to heaven appeared with a mallet in his hand and held it out for Al to take. At the same moment, the juke-box directly behind Al kicked into gear. Al could hear the voices of John G. Erie and Hope Himmelmann in the strategy meeting Al had relived before with Adrian. "Be my guest." Frank grinned and stepped back. Al approached the jukebox.

"John G. Erie is trying to get us to think differently," Hope's voice screeched through the machine. He raised the mallet as she continued to drone on about mollusks and octopuses. Al vaguely remembered wondering whether she should have said "octopi." Al raised the mallet, and then, inexplicably, he began laughing. It started as a light laugh but soon erupted into a good old-fashioned belly-heaving laugh, and by the time Al turned to Frank, he was laughing just as hard.

"Forget it," Al said, lowering the mallet and handing it back to the puzzled cherub. "It's not worth it. I don't care anymore."

"Send this man back out into the world!" Frank shouted to no one in particular. "He's cured!"

℃ Within the moment, Al could smell the pungently sweet aroma so familiar in his youth—the blooming Korean spice bushes in his mother's garden. He was walking along the familiar brick path, the white blooming orchids on either side of him. He could see the back of the house, a modest yellow split-level ranch, the back door open as it always seemed to be when he was a boy. The Mitchells were outside people after all, and from what Al could tell, the weather on this day—whatever day it was—was beautiful, meaning his father would be tinkering with the car in the driveway and his mother would be tending to her colorful and fragrant plantings. Al grew up loving the garden, though he could never admit as much, since boys in his neighborhood were too tough to like those kinds of things. Al climbed the back stairs—the middle step creaked like it always did—and stepped into the narrow mudroom, where, as a child, he always took off his shoes. The washer and dryer were there, the coat hooks, the shoe shelf, and the black rubber mat with the words *For Feet Only* scripted across it. Al continued through the mudroom and entered the kitchen, where a feeling of comfort and warmth overtook him completely. The kitchen wasn't very big, but it was consistently bright, thanks to the large windows and the skylight. Al was amazed at the little details coming back to him about this room where he had eaten so many meals, completed his homework in grammar school, and at a very young age he could barely recall, spun pot lids on the floor for fun. There was the old-fashioned egg timer on top of the stove, the ambulance-shaped magnet on the refrigerator with emergency phone numbers, the rhythmic tick-tock of the pendulum clock in the dining room. There was a little nook for the kitchen table in the corner. Chet Harbourton was sitting at the table alone, his hands folded as if in prayer.

"Do you know who I am?" Al asked.

Chet responded with a blank stare.

"Do you know who I am?" Al repeated.

"I know who you are," Chet said, rubbing his hands together, betraying his discomfort and nervousness. "I think this is a dream."

"Maybe," Al responded. "What I don't know is if you are in my dream or I am in yours. I do know that this is the house I grew up in."

"A very nice house," Chet said.

Having originally planned to give Harbourton a very explicit piece of his mind for his lax maintenance practices, Al instead found that the warm feeling washing over him was growing more deep and more intense, and that he could not work up any anger toward the man sitting at his table. Frankie T. Mayhem's MAD program must have worked.

"You know what's funny?" Al walked to the table to get a better look at Harbourton. "No matter how old I got, or how many other places I lived, in every one of my dreams, I always lived in this house."

"A very nice house," Chet repeated. "Your parents provided good for you."

"Yes, they did."

"You were lucky. I only knew my mama," Chet looked out the window reflectively, then turned to look Al right in the eye. "I prayed to the Lord for a chance to see you and to speak to you. And now that the Lord has granted my request"—he hesitated, composing himself—"I don't know what to say to you."

"There is nothing you have to say." Al was disarmed by the man's approach but tried to convey a cheeriness that he knew must have sounded awkward and probably not genuine.

"At least . . ." Chet began to cry. "At least, I can say . . . I'm sorry," he finished through the sobs.

"I asked to talk to you, too," Al said, sitting down. "There was something I wanted to say to you." Chet looked up, using his hands to brush away the tears and at the same time hide his quivering lips. Al spoke slowly, reassuringly. "Don't blame yourself. It was an accident."

"But I was responsible!" Chet slammed his hands on the table.

Al immediately grabbed them. "You were no more at fault than the guy who was running the ride or wrote the software program."

Chet listened, but his face remained tense. "I can't face my children knowing I did something that killed a man!"

"Your kids will know what you tell them, Chet! They've heard everybody say it was an accident. They need to hear it from you. I want you to tell them it was an accident."

"You do?" Chet looked up hopefully.

"Yes, I do. For the sake of your children, don't go hide away for the rest of your life like you are a criminal. Because if you do, that's what your children will think you are. And they deserve more than that from you!"

Chet bit his lip for a few moments and looked out the window again. "Do you . . . Did you have kids?"

"No!" Al said emphatically. "Don't worry about that." His spirit waned a bit as he continued. "I had no kids . . . no wife. No family to speak of. Not much of an epitaph, is it?"

"I'm sorry about that," Chet said.

"Don't be. Look at it this way: You did me a favor. You sent me to a place where I am better off. I am no longer going to worry about what I screwed up or didn't do in the past, and just focus on having a great afterlife! You need to go back and have dinner with your wife and kids . . . tonight . . . tomorrow night . . . every night. Don't do to them what your father did to you."

"I'll pray for you every day," Chet said.

Tears welled in Al's eyes as he stood up, blurring his vision. By the time he wiped them away, Harbourton was gone. Adrian was standing next to him.

"That felt pretty good," Al said to no one in particular.

"Are we done with Mr. Harbourton?" Adrian asked solemnly.

"Yeah." Al swallowed hard and wiped away one more tear. "We are."

Adrian put his arm around Al and gave him a look of admiration.

"Well done, my friend," Adrian said warmly.

No sooner had Adrian finished complementing Al than they found themselves in the refreshing heavenly outdoors where they had started. The sun was warm but not hot, the breeze was strong enough to ruffle but not bend the tall wisps of grass, and the scent of the blooming bushes reminded Al of his mother's garden. Al stood quietly and took it all in, much more appreciative of it.

"This is so beautiful," Al said. "I'm going to love it here." Adrian was about to answer, but a birdlike chirping caught his attention. He pulled out his HEAVEN box. A red light on the console was blinking furiously.

"What's the matter?" Al asked.

"Urgent message," Adrian said. "First time I've ever gotten one." Adrian opened the box and studied the screen quickly, then shut the box.

"Everything okay?"

Adrian looked uncomfortable and winced.

"Not quite," he said. "About your getting into heaven . . ." he started, and then paused. Al did not like the look on Adrian's face.

"What about my getting into heaven? We're done with HARP. I get into heaven now, don't I?"

"Not quite," Adrian replied again.

"There he goes with the 'not quite' again." Al eyed him suspiciously. "You said when HARP was over, I would get all the rights and privileges of heaven."

Adrian smiled, embarrassed.

"I know. But something unexpected has come up."

CHAPTER 16

rights and privileges

A DRIAN WAS PACING nervously with Al hot on his tail.

"What do you mean something has come up? I'm supposed to get my rights and privileges now."

Adrian turned, his face tightening.

"That was before this latest news I just received. I'm afraid you can't obtain your rights and privileges at this time," he said.

"Why not?"

Adrian fidgeted with something inside his jacket pocket, finally pulling out a fist-sized box made of bronze. He opened it and fished out a red pennant-shaped sticker and pressed it onto Al's shirt.

"Sorry, Al. You've been flagged."

"What?" Al screeched.

"Someone just flagged you as a jerk." Adrian returned the box to his pocket and scratched his head, his voice remaining measured. "I was never good at giving bad news to people, but I suppose it's part of my job now." He looked Al square in the eye. "When was the last time you talked to your ex-wife?"

"Liz? I don't know. It's been years."

"Did you know she had been very sick?"

"No!" Al looked genuinely surprised.

"You may want to brace yourself for this," Adrian said as he lowered his eyes. "She passed from the earth this morning."

"Liz died?" Al asked through a strong shudder of sadness.

"I'm afraid so." Adrian sighed.

"I knew I should have talked to her. . . ." His voice trailed off.

"Don't feel too bad, Al. The good news is, her suffering is over and she's up here with us. The bad news is, as soon as she arrived, she flagged you as one of the five jerks in her life. Your full rights and privileges will be suspended until after you answer her charges. If you answer them well, you can walk right through the pearly gates. If you don't, then you will have to perform a prescribed penance before your rights and privileges are restored."

Al turned away. A thousand moments with Liz flashed by as he tried to absorb the news. Adrian was right—he should feel good that she had come to a better place—but for the moment, he could not get over a massive surge of guilt that he could neither control nor explain.

"Can I see her?" he asked.

"You will—very shortly—at the hearing."

"What hearing?"

"The hearing to weigh her charges . . . We're going there now."

"Now?" Al was suddenly panicked. "I'm not ready. . . ."

"There's nothing to prepare for. Just be honest, and everything will turn out all right." Adrian could see his advice did not comfort Al. "If you want, I'll stay there with you." Al enthusiastically nodded his assent as a frightening thought crept into his head.

"This hearing . . . It isn't in front of—" he hesitated—"you know. . . ."

"You mean God?" Adrian completed the sentence for him. "Of course not. He's got much bigger fish to fry than determining whether you and your wife were having-and-holding-until-you-did-part."

"Then who presides over the hearing?"

"THEY do."

"Who do?"

"THEY—The Heavenly Enlightened Yea-sayers," Adrian answered, as if the information should be obvious.

"Is this pig Latin or an Abbott and Costello routine?"

"You need to get faster on the uptake, Al. THEY are a panel heaven put together made up of the great minds and enlightened intellects in history—the ones everybody quotes when they need a clever saying or maxim."

Al still looked puzzled.

"You know"—Adrian was getting impatient—"'THEY say you shouldn't put the cart before the horse' or 'You know what THEY say, a penny saved is a penny earned!'"

It finally clicked for Al.

"You mean there is a real THEY?"

"Of course, there is a real THEY."

"I always thought THEY were just part of the expression."

"Nope. THEY are a real group of people." Adrian lowered his voice to a whisper. "Just between you and me, I think THEY are a bunch of doddering old busybodies, always trying to show how smart THEY are with their wise old sayings."

"You don't like them?" Al asked.

"Don't call THEY them, Al. Ever since that movie about the giant ants came out, THEY have been very sensitive about being called them. THEY are also a little sensitive about the acronym, as you'll see."

"I was kind of wondering about that. What is a yea-sayer?"

"It's a real word. It's in the dictionary." Adrian opened the trusty HEAVEN box and the word appeared on the screen along with a definition. "One whose attitude is that of confident affirmation," Adrian read.

"That seems like a stretch."

"Oh, it is," Adrian confirmed. "But *Y* is a hard letter to use in an acronym. It was the best THEY could do."

"How do I deal with them—THEY?" Al quickly corrected himself.

"Just show how much you think THEY are wise and all-knowing. Quote a lot of THEY sayings. THEY like that."

November 1879

Ezekiel Cornwallower owned the three-story Greek Revival mansion that his neighbors called the jewel of the Hudson for its architectural beauty and for the way the late-day sun would glimmer off its stained-glass windows. Mr. Cornwallower was a local-boy-made-

good who left the lush Hudson River Valley region for
the thirty-mile trip down the river to New York City
when he was only fourteen. Learning his way as he
went, Cornwallower became a millionaire in the building
supply business during the postwar reconstruction of
the Confederate states, when it was almost a national
sport to overcharge southern interests for the commodi-
ties they needed to get back on their feet.

He built the three-story Greek Revival mansion his
neighbors so admired in 1871. However, without the
captive and desperate south as market for his goods,
and with a recession hitting in mid-decade, Cornwallower
came up broke by 1879.

Now, here he was on a gray day, wrapped against
an ill November wind, helping his frail wife into the
horse carriage that would take them to their new, more
modest quarters in Connecticut. Neighbors, friends, and
curious members of the press, who had always counted
on the dynamic businessman for a good quote, watched
the drama unfold. As Cornwallower pulled his rotund
self into the carriage, a smattering of applause broke
out in the group, and Cornwallower turned, removed
his top hat, and bowed courteously.

One of the press men nearby asked how he felt
about selling his beautiful mansion. Replacing his hat
with a bit of a rakish tilt, Cornwallower yelled to the
crowd, "You know what THEY say . . . easy come,
easy go!" A trail of approving laughter followed the
Cornwallower carriage down the stone driveway.

THEY convened all deliberations in the sad remains of the Cornwallower mansion, which still sat at the end of a forgotten spur off the roads running along the cliffs above the Hudson River. Once the standard for elegance among the eastern U.S. gentry, it was now a dilapidated hollow shell slowly being lashed apart by the brutal elements of the New York weather. THEY chose this location in tribute to Mr. Cornwallower's clever reply to the reporter as he left his mansion, the first-ever instance of someone citing the wisdom of THEY.

Al and Adrian found themselves standing in this ghost of a mansion, in what must have once been a magnificent foyer. It reached to the third-story roof, where a large hole was all that remained of a stained-glass window. Only about half of the grand staircase still stood. At one time it swirled completely around the foyer, reaching to the third floor. Now it barely reached the framework that once supported the second floor. The stairs ended directly under the fragments of chains that hinted at the huge chandelier that once dangled there. The rest of the building was all crumbling walls and sprouting weeds. If there was one good thing about the dilapidated state of the mansion, it was that the many holes and missing walls allowed for a breathtaking view of the magnificent vista of the Hudson River Valley below.

Suddenly a pleasant but authoritative voice washed over the foyer. "Al Mitchell," it called out.

"I'm here," Al shouted, looking around.

Whether he had been there all along or not, Al could not say, but there was a man on the top of the staircase. He started down the stairs completely oblivious to the battered and dangerous conditions around him. As he descended, a second man appeared at the top step, and as he descended, a third appeared, and so on until nine men had appeared and were making their way down the steps. As each man reached the foyer, a raised podium appeared for him on which sat a high-backed leather chair behind a wood panel. The panel boasted a manicured gold letter. The first podium had the letter *Y* and the second an *E*. When all nine podiums appeared, the individual letters would merge to spell *YEASAYERS*. As the ninth podium appeared, the first of the men down the stairs approached Al and Adrian. He walked with the soft, confident gait of an old-world gentleman, an air of calm and sophistication about him. He was stout and bald, with pleasant eyes and an impressive white beard. In contrast to his formal manner, he wore casual jeans and a yellow T-shirt with bold lettering across the front that read "Yes, Yea-sayer is a real word." His eight compatriots were similarly dressed, and as the men took their designated podium seat, Al scanned through the messages on their T-shirts:

"Yea-sayers do it better."

"Better yea-sayer than nay-sayer."

"Just say 'yea.'"

"Hug a yea-sayer today."

"We're looking for a few good yea-sayers."

"Yea-sayers are the 'why' in 'THEY.'"

"Believe everything THEY tell you."

"Kiss me, I'm a yea-sayer."

"I see what you mean about this yea-sayer thing," Al said, hoping his sense of humor would help him control his growing nervousness. Adrian elbowed him to be quiet.

"Albert Mitchell?" The bearded man had a soft, airy voice colored with a British accent.

"Here, sir," Al said nervously.

"Good." The old man turned to Adrian. "You may go."

"I would ask permission to stay," Adrian said respectfully.

"Why?" The gentleman tugged thoughtfully at his beard.

"You know what THEY say." Adrian smiled. "A friend in need is a friend indeed. I would like to stay with my friend, indeed."

The bearded man chuckled and turned to his companions seated behind him. "Pluto!" he said with a hint of playfulness. "You've just been quoted!" The man in the first seat half-rose and saluted Adrian thankfully.

"That's Plutarch," the bearded man said. "He wrote some of the greatest essays and biographies in the ancient Greek world, but he gets a bigger kick when someone uses one of his sayings." He lowered his voice, as if speaking in confidence. "We call him Pluto because he has come to like cartoons so much." He then turned solemn again and faced Adrian.

"You can stay," he said, "but Mr. Mitchell must represent himself." He turned to Al. "You do understand that?"

"Yes."

"Good. My name is Charles"—he politely bowed—"and my colleagues and I are here to represent THEY."

"So, if I am me, and you are THEY, and we are all together . . . who is the Walrus?" Al cracked. He shot a quick glance at a horrified Adrian and quickly wiped away his grin when he saw the stony response of the old man. "Sorry. Never mind," Al whispered. Charles shook his head as if concerned.

"Sometimes I wonder how humans survived natural selection," he said to Adrian exasperatedly.

"It wasn't a very good joke, Mr. Darwin," Adrian said.

"You're Charles Darwin?" Al said, horrified. "I'm sorry. I didn't know. I'm sorry about the joke, sir. I admired your work. I read *On the Origin of Species* in college."

"Yes, well, I would call your joke *On the Origin of Feces*." Darwin turned to his colleagues, who broke out in uninhibited laughter.

"I'm sorry, Mr. Darwin," Adrian said as the laughter ebbed. "Mr. Mitchell is new—"

"I know that," Darwin interrupted Adrian. "Does he understand this hearing and what is expected of him?"

"Yes, sir. I explained everything to him."

"Good." Darwin turned to Al. "Sometimes all that nonsense people are told on earth gets in the way up here. People are always asking questions like 'Where are your wings' and all that rot."

"Wings?" Al pretended to laugh. "Don't people know how aerodynamically unsound wings are on a human body?"

"Quite," Darwin responded, more pleased with this observation from Al. "Now, to the matter at hand. Your former wife was very displeased with you during her time on earth. She has accused you of being one of the five jerks she met in her life."

"I know," Al said, a trace of regret in his voice. "Adrian told me."

"We will hear her claims and your response and be done with this quickly." He turned his head and called out, "Elizabeth Buckman Mitchell!" There was the soft patter of light footsteps on the marble floor of the foyer, and Liz came into view.

The details of her features as Al remembered them had changed. Her face was very smooth and, much like Adrian's, had lost whatever features might have made it easier to guess her age: the wrinkles on her brow, gone; the crow's feet that Al had noticed last time he had seen her, gone as well. Her hair had lost the strands of white and now radiated a luminous black sheen. Her manner and her motion suggested a simple comfort and pleasantness.

"Hi, Liz," Al said a bit sheepishly.

Before responding, Liz looked to Darwin, who nodded approvingly. "You can speak to him." He smiled.

"Okay." Liz turned to Al. "This is all so new to me; I don't know what the rules allow. How are you, Al?"

"Just fine. I guess you are now, too."

"Yes. I feel wonderful."

"I'm sorry I didn't know you were so sick."

Liz laughed. "That would be the perfect summary of our marriage. You didn't know."

"We should begin," Darwin said. "Are you comfortable with these surroundings?"

"Not entirely," Liz answered politely. "This place is so run down . . . so depressing. Can we go to the boardwalk?"

No sooner were the words out of her mouth than everyone was at the Seafarer Boardwalk, sitting on a set of benches overlooking the ocean. It was an unhappy-looking day—thick clouds pushed low on the horizon and the normally crisp blue water was a dull, depressing gray. A fog was building and the gathering gloom accentuated the myriad neon lights running atop the stores and game booths. Although they were the only souls to be seen, the noises associated with a crowded day filled the air.

"This was my favorite bench," Liz said. "I could watch the ocean and the waves for hours."

"Really?" Al was genuinely surprised.

"Yes, really!" She turned to Darwin. "Just the fact he didn't know that speaks volumes," Liz said, refocusing on Al. "We could never just sit and enjoy the day . . . enjoy the surroundings."

"You never suggested it," Al said defensively.

"I shouldn't have had to," Liz snapped back.

Adrian leaned over and whispered in Al's ear. "You lost that round, my friend."

"Then," Liz continued, "we always had to go to that rickety old bar at the other end of the pier. You would choke to death on the foul smell of the stale beer and cigarettes. Most of the people in there were just old drunks getting older and drunker."

"You should have told me. . . ." Al said defensively.

"I shouldn't have had to," Liz came back again sharply.

Adrian grimaced and leaned toward Al's ear again. "That's Round Two, kid. If you say, 'You should have told me,' one more time this fight will be a third-round knockout."

"And then there was that stupid merry-go-round ride and his stupid horse!" Liz said almost venomously. "We had to go on that stupid ride every time we were down here. I didn't mind once in a while, but it was all the time! I wanted to give that horse a one-way ticket to the glue factory."

"You always said you liked the ride!" Al pleaded.

"What was I going to say?" Liz snapped. "That the ride was stupid and you were stupid for being so obsessed with it?"

"I can't read your mind!" Al shot back.

"You shouldn't have to! If you talked with me sometimes, you would have known! That's what married people do! They know each other's likes and dislikes and they don't have to pretend with each other!"

Adrian raised his right hand like an umpire. "And that's strike three!"

"Oh, shut up," Al snapped at him. "Go sit with her, why don't you?"

"Does the sum total of your complaints reside with the fact Al was not aware of your likes and dislikes on the boardwalk"? Darwin asked Liz.

"No," Liz said, more measured. "That was an example of our problems. Al was a man of great energy and passion for everything in his life. Then, little by little, his passion was channeled to his job and other things. He would miss family events and be late for important occasions. Why? Because of work. He would get home long after dinner most every night because of work. There was a time when he used to tell me jokes and make me laugh almost every day. Little by little, the jokes stopped. Then the laughter stopped. You don't know how much I missed laughing."

Adrian turned to Liz.

"If you need a good laugh, ask Al how he died."

Al gave Adrian a Ralph Kramden–like whack on the shoulder.

"Gentlemen, please," Darwin admonished, then turned politely to Liz. "Is there anything else you would like to tell us as to why your husband is a jerk?"

"He's a jerk because we could have had a good marriage . . . a great marriage. But his passion for it went away. I don't know why. I don't know what I did. But for no reason at all, he just stopped working at it. He just stopped trying."

Darwin turned to Al.

"I will give you a few minutes to compose yourself and your response." Darwin walked over to his compatriots sitting on the adjacent benches. They stood in a football-like huddle, some of them occasionally stealing a condemning look at Al.

"You're lucky this is only a hearing and not a murder trial," Adrian said. "Otherwise, I think they'd give you a week in the electric chair."

"I didn't know they made such a big production out of this," Liz said, more in admiration than embarrassment. "Tell me." She cuddled up to Adrian. "What did you mean before about Al dying?"

"I had an accident," Al cut in.

"A car accident?" she asked.

"No. I was thrown from a horse."

Adrian tried to stifle a laugh.

"Oh, my God!" Liz eyed him sadly. "When did you take up horseback riding?" She turned to Adrian. "He took up horseback riding?"

"Not exactly." Adrian waved her to come closer. He whispered in her ear as Al sat fuming.

"He did what?" she blurted out loud. By the time Darwin returned to the bench and THEY had taken their seats, Adrian and Liz were both doubled over, laughing hysterically.

Charles Darwin ignored their antics and addressed Al.

"What have you to say in response?"

"It's always tough to balance work responsibilities and home life. It seemed to me like advancing my career and making sure we had enough money to live a good life was my primary responsibility and I took it seriously."

"Is it not every man's responsibility to find that balance?" Darwin asked imperiously.

"I suppose so." Al's response came reluctantly, and he caught sight of Adrian shaking his head again.

"You did not do that, did you?" Darwin said.

"No," Al said softly.

"What did you say?" Darwin demanded.

"No!" Al said more emphatically.

Darwin studied Al with no trace of sympathy.

"Where was your passion, young man?"

"It was . . . around," Al said weakly.

"Great answer," Adrian said under his breath.

"Would it be fair to say your continuing elevation of responsibilities and stature at your place of work caused you to continually renew your passion for the work?" Darwin asked.

"Yes, I suppose so."

"And did you bring an equal amount of renewed passion to elevate your marital relationship?"

"I don't know. I tried," Al said softly.

Darwin stared at him coldly.

"Wait here a moment, please," he said, returning to talk with his colleagues.

"How am I doing?" Al asked Adrian.

"Good, if you don't count everything you've said so far."

THEY broke their short conference and this time all of the men walked over with Darwin and encircled the bench.

"We would like you to follow us, young man." THEY led Al a short way down the boardwalk and to the arcade, with Liz and Adrian in tow. First they passed the Wheel of Fortune-Tellers, then, once inside the arcade, the video games, the poker machines, and the picture-taking booths. Darwin halted the parade in front of the old-fashioned Test Your Strength attraction, where patrons swing down a mallet on a lever at the base of the machine, causing a weight on the other end of the lever to go flying up a tower. The stronger the user, the higher up the tower the weight will go, with the ultimate aim being to ring the bell at the top of the tower. Darwin picked up the mallet and handed it to Al, who tested the weight by balancing it in both hands.

"What are we doing this for?" Al asked politely.

"Your performance on this machine will help us decide."

"You're going to decide based on how strong I am? I don't get it."

"You don't need to at the moment," Darwin said, as though addressing a know-it-all student at one of his lectures.

"I used to be able to ring the bell nearly every time." Al raised the mallet like a bat and struck a baseball-card-like pose.

"You may make up to three tries," Darwin said, stepping back.

"Okay!" Al wiped his hands as dry as he could get them, loosened up his neck, raised the mallet to his shoulder, and approached his target. He judged the tower to be about twelve feet high. Each foot of the tower was a different color, beginning with black on the bottom, gray for the second foot, white for the third, and two tints each of green, blue, yellow, and red taking it up to eleven feet, with the bell representing the remaining foot.

"Pretend it's Butch Lowe," Adrian urged him.

Al planted his feet firmly, took a deep breath, and brought the mallet down on the lever with all of his strength. The mallet hit with what seemed an impressive force, but the weight in the tower barely nudged upward. It did not clear the first foot.

"One of us is rusty," Al said to the machine.

"Nice shot," Adrian said caustically. "The Munchkins can hit it higher than that. Maybe you can clear your shoe tops on the next one."

Al clasped the mallet harder and gave Adrian a you-are-not-helping look, then he brought it up high over his head and tried again. The weight edged slightly higher but was still in the black zone—the first foot.

"What happened to my he-man?" Liz grinned.

"You do realize the idea is to make the weight go up?" Adrian asked. "Maybe you want to get a running start this time?"

It wasn't Adrian's jokes as much as Liz's laughing at them that was getting Al steamed. Fantasizing that the mallet was Adrian's neck, he gripped the handle hard enough to squeeze out sawdust and then brought it down with as much force as he possibly could: The weight edged between the gray and white colors. Darwin reached for the mallet and took it from Al.

"Something is wrong with that thing," Al said. "Is this a joke or something?"

"No," the old man said solemnly, handing the mallet to Liz. "Would you take one shot at it, please?"

"Sure." Liz shrugged, gripping the mallet and bringing it down on the lever without so much as a pause. The weight shot up the tower and rang the bell.

"Nothing to it." Liz handed the mallet to Darwin.

"This is a setup." Al turned to Adrian. "You set this up as a joke, didn't you." Adrian shook his head quickly, his look urging Al not to anger THEY.

"This is not a joke." Darwin took the mallet from Liz. "I'm afraid, Albert, that we have to rule in favor of your wife and what she has told us," the old man said.

"How can you do that?" Al was perturbed. "Based on this silly machine?"

"We found out all we need to know by your performance just now."

"How does testing my strength tell you what you want to know?"

"This machine does not test your strength," the old man cut in. "No. This machine measures your passion. The colors on the tower represent increasing and intensifying passion as you go upward. You have black, gray, and white on the bottom. They represent essentially an absence of passion. Your wife said it was an absence of passion for her and for the marriage . . . a lack of passion for the things required to make the marriage work. Based on your anemic attempts at ringing the bell, I must say that she was right. Her claim that you were a jerk is upheld."

Al linked eyes with his former wife. She looked at him sympathetically, without disdain or hint of satisfaction. He tried to reassure her with a smile, but it was tough. His had been an embarrassingly weak defense, but in his heart he knew why—because everything Liz had said was right.

"I'm sorry," Liz said to him. "I really believed what I said to be true."

"It was true," Al conceded to her, then turned to THEY. "If I'm going to have a great afterlife, I'm going to start by being honest with everyone, beginning with myself. Liz was right. The machine was right. I never put into the marriage what I should have. I never believed the marriage would last in the long run. I think about some of the people in my life—the Butch Lowes and the Morgan Telfords—and it seems like everybody who had the chance to screw me over took full advantage of it. To me, life was a paper route and there was always a Butch Lowe coming around the corner to steal anything worthwhile.

"Much as I loved Liz"—he turned to her—"and I did love her, I couldn't fully trust the marriage. I was always sure something bad was going to come out of it. I guess I fulfilled my own prophecy. I am sorry." She started crying and he turned back to THEY. "I should have done things differently. But I didn't." He shrugged. "You know what THEY say, hindsight is 20/20."

"Actually, we did not say that," Darwin said politely. "THOSE said that."

"Who?" Al asked.

"THOSE—The Heavenly Order of Sage Experts. They are a different panel, and if you permit me a moment of frankness, they are made up of pretend intellects and second-rate philosophers like that Karl Marx fellow . . . ones who thought themselves qualified for THEY and when they were rejected, went ahead and formed THOSE on their own. They are quite a humorless group . . . unimaginative . . . a bit stodgy, if you ask me. Please take care not to mix up THEY and THOSE in the future."

Al stared dumbfounded. Heaven was going to be tougher to get used to than he ever imagined.

"You realize you have conceded to your wife's accusations?" Darwin asked.

"Yes."

Darwin cracked a big smile.

"Good show, old man!" he beamed at Al and patted him on the shoulder. "I like an honest man . . . a man who can admit to his shortcomings. Of course, if a man is too well practiced in admitting his shortcomings, then he has too many shortcomings and I shan't like him, so it is a bit of a quandary, isn't it? But not for you to worry about."

He turned to Liz.

"Thank you, Elizabeth. Your rights and privileges are waiting for you. You can go."

Liz smiled at Al, still wiping the tears away. "Will you come see me after your penance?"

"I'll make sure he does," Adrian replied for him.

"Good." Liz gave Adrian a wink and they shared one last guffaw over Al's mishap. She thanked THEY before turning to Al, looking at him for only a few moments before tearing up again. "Bye," she said weakly to him.

Al waved to her, not knowing what to say. He could feel the eighteen eyes of THEY peering down on him as he watched her walk away. There had certainly not been any passion in his good-bye.

"Can I have a minute alone?" Al asked Darwin, who nodded politely. Al rushed to catch up with his former wife, grabbing her by the elbow and walking her in front of Miss Fortune.

"Are you mad at me?" she said mischievously.

"I didn't name you as one of my five jerks, you know," Al said self-righteously.

"Why didn't you?" Liz asked.

"Because . . ."

"You should have!" Liz's placidity was turning to anger and she began pounding him on the chest. "Every single divorced person who comes up here names their ex-spouse. *Except you!* I'm the only wife you ever had! I'm married to you for more than fifteen years, and you don't think I'm as important as Dean James or that trollop Morgan Telford! You *should* have named me one of your jerks! The fact you didn't makes you an even *bigger jerk*!"

"Okay, I'm sorry." Al threw his hands up, as if surrendering. "Believe me, any chance I get from now through eternity, I will make sure I tell everyone what a big jerk you were."

"You better not." Liz grinned, hitting him again, only this time playfully. "Or I'll tell everyone in heaven how you died!" For the first time in a longer time than either of them could remember, they shared a laugh. Liz wrapped her arms around him and gave him a gentle kiss on the cheek.

"Go do your penance," she said. They shared a final silent moment together before she walked away, disappearing in the fog of that gloomy day. He rejoined Adrian and THEY.

"I'm ready," Al said to Darwin.

"Based on current circumstances"—Darwin put his arm on Al's shoulder—"I should think your penance will be fairly light."

"Thank you," Al said. Darwin turned to Adrian. "Your penance is now complete, is it not, Adrian?"

"Yes," Adrian said.

"Good. Let us have Albert follow in your footsteps. First, give Al the hope he needs to do his penance correctly."

"I will," Adrian said, pulling the *H* off the jacket of his suit. Adrian walked over and placed the *H* on Al's shirt. "The *H* stands for 'Hope,'" Adrian said to Al. "All penitents wear it. Helps to remind you what heaven is all about."

"Good, Adrian," Darwin said. "Your penance is complete. Well done."

"You were doing penance?" Al asked.

"Yes," Adrian admitted, opening his jacket. One of those red pennant-shaped stickers was on his shirt. "I was flagged as a jerk just like you were."

"What did you do?"

"It's a long story."

"Tell it. You never did tell me anything about yourself."

"On earth, I ran numbers."

"You mean a bookie?"

"No. I was a quantum mechanical mathematician. Of course, I was a bookie," Adrian said. "I ran numbers out of south Philadelphia for thirty years."

"How does a bookie become an angel?" Al asked incredulously.

"See?" Adrian's voice rose as he launched into another of his rants. "There you go again! First it's 'Oh, Adrian, you don't look like an angel.' Now it's 'Oh, Adrian, how can you be an angel?' Why can't I be an angel? I make just as good an angel as anybody!"

"Calm down," Darwin urged. "You're a fine angel."

Adrian caught himself, realizing he was in front of THEY.

"Okay, sorry. It's a sore point with me. Becoming a bookie was what I had to do to survive. My parents were dead by the time I was fifteen and my brother died in the war. I was alone on the streets. This guy from the Italian section, Lena Toweropiza, knew me because I used to deliver groceries to his mother. He started giving me a few jobs here and there . . . running numbers . . . collecting for him. I made enough money to eat. When I got old enough, I went into business for myself with Lena's blessing. I did pretty well for myself for thirty years and I'm not ashamed of it."

"How did you get flagged?" Al asked.

"I was a peaceful guy. Thirty years in my own business and I never so much as scratched anybody. But Lena . . . he did some work for the mob . . . rough work. He hurt some people, one of them pretty bad. When that guy got to heaven, he fingered Lena as a jerk for hurting him, and me because I had introduced the two of them at a ball game."

Darwin put his arm around Adrian like a proud father would on graduation day.

"We had Adrian do penance by requiring him to help a new arrival with HARP. Turned out it was you," Darwin explained.

"Now I'm done and it's your turn." Adrian patted the *H* now firmly attached to Al's shirt.

"Albert, you, too, will now help a new arrival with HARP. Help someone get restitution against five jerks. When that is completed, you will have earned your rights and privileges," Darwin said.

"I'm ready to go," Al said enthusiastically. "I have to say that all of this has helped me wash out of my soul what people like Butch Lowe and Morgan Telford did to me." Al broke into the broadest grin the confines of his face would allow. "It's amazing how happy I feel right now."

"That's what HARP is truly all about." Darwin beamed. "It may seem as though it is about vengeance, but it is really about lifting burdens."

"Thanks to Adrian," Al said. "I can't believe how much I learned from him in such a short time." Al looked Adrian right in the eye. "I think you turned out to be the best friend I have ever had."

Adrian was touched. Then he grinned. "Based on what I saw of your life, that's not much of a compliment. But thanks anyway." They embraced warmly and exchanged thankful glances. Adrian gave Al a thumbs-up and peeled off the red sticker.

"I'll see you when you get back," he said, and turned to walk off.

"I would hate to lose such a great source of information and such a great teacher," Al appealed to Darwin.

"Would you mind holding up for a moment, Adrian?" Darwin asked. "I've been thinking about what Albert suggested." Adrian turned, casting a suspicious eye on Al. "I think it would be a good idea for us to institute a mentoring program for new arrivals." Darwin turned to his colleagues. "Don't you think it would be an excellent idea?" Each of them nodded his enthusiastic approval. We could designate it Heavenly Angel Mentoring . . . HAM!" He thought for a moment and wrinkled his nose. "Maybe not." He turned to Adrian. "We will come up with a better acronym. What do you think?"

"A very good idea," Adrian said hesitantly. "If you don't mind, I think I will go and have my rights and privileges instituted."

"Nonsense, old boy!" Darwin grabbed him by the arm.

"Adrian would be a great mentor." Al grabbed his other arm. Adrian etched a painful smile on his face to mask his annoyance at Al. "I think Adrian should be the first mentor angel. He can mentor me!"

"An excellent idea!" Darwin and THEY murmured their approval.

"But I just got my rights and privileges again. . . ."

"Oh rot." Darwin laughed. "Surely if you've waited this long, Adrian, a little longer won't hurt you. Do you agree?"

"Wholeheartedly," Adrian said with a tone that was anything but. THEY broke out in applause.

"And I am sure you also agree that mentoring is an excellent idea and that you will want to be our very first mentor angel!"

"I am honored beyond words," Adrian said flatly.

"Good show!" Darwin beamed.

Al, who had joined in the applause, gave his new mentor a pat on the back. "You know what THEY say, there is nothing more powerful than an idea whose time has come."

Darwin let out a throaty laugh. "Indeed!" he said, pointing to one of his colleagues in the back of the group. "And there is Mr. Hugo now. Victor!" he called out. "There is another notch for your belt!"

Darwin shook hands with Al, then turned to Adrian again and gave him a hug. He maneuvered his head to whisper into Adrian's ear. "Not bad for a doddering old busybody, don't you think?" Darwin pulled back to give him a vengeful smile. "Remember," he said aloud, "once you get to heaven, the clouds have ears!"

Darwin joined his laughing colleagues and they began filing out of the arcade and back into eternity.

Adrian gave Al the dirtiest look allowed in heaven. "You and Mr. Darwin thought of this together?"

"You could say the idea evolved from Darwin."

"What am I supposed to do now?"

"Mentor me!" Al said overenthusiastically. "Come on, Mr. Mentor Angel! I need you to be faster on the uptake!"

"Shut up," Adrian said.

The End—

which is just another beginning . . .